$S \cdot O \cdot U \cdot N \cdot D$ SEASONINGS

The Junior League of Westchester on the Sound

The Junior League is an organization of women committed to promoting voluntarism and to improving the community through the effective action and leadership of trained volunteers. Its purpose is exclusively educational and charitable.

Proceeds from the sale of SOUND SEASONINGS will be returned to the community through the projects of the Junior League of Westchester on the Sound, Inc.

First Printing   May 1990   10,000 Copies

If you wish to order additional copies of SOUND SEASONINGS, please use the order blanks provided in the back of the book, or write to:

The Junior League of Westchester on the Sound, Inc.
P.O. Box 765
Larchmont, New York 10538

Printed by
WIMMER BROTHERS
A Wimmer Company
Memphis • Dallas

Acknowledgements

Cover Art
Ronnie Wadler is an art teacher and shows her work regularly in national juried shows; she is also currently working as a children's book illustrator. She holds a Masters degree in Fine Arts from the University of Wisconsin. Mrs. Wadler lives in Larchmont, New York, with her husband and two children.

Cover Design
Andrew Newman is principal of Andrew M. Newman Graphic Design, Inc., of New York City, a firm specializing in promotional materials and corporate design. He is an active member of national and New York graphic arts organizations. His work has been shown and won awards in the Desi Show, Creativity, Humor 87 and American Corporate Identity 6. Mr. Newman and his family are residents of Larchmont.

Introduction and Herb Primer
Ellen H. Parlapiano, a former editor at Women's Day Special Interest Magazines, is a free-lance writer who frequently covers food, nutrition, child care and parenting topics. She lives in Scarsdale, New York.

Local Illustrations
Grace Huntley Pugh, Art Advisor to the Village of Mamaroneck, has been painting Westchester County for more than 50 years. A member of the American Watercolor Society and first president of the Mamaroneck Artists Guild, she has exhibited oils and watercolors in more than 50 solo shows and her paintings are in numerous public and private collections. She studied at Wellesley College, received a Bachelor of Fine Arts from Barnard College, and studied at the National Academy of Design and the Art Students League.

The committee wishes to acknowledge the following League volunteers whose valuable guidance and expertise helped to make this book a reality: Joan Macfarlane, writing consultant; Rebecca Reisman, contributing writer of the historical notes; Dorothy Robertshaw, design consultant; and our own committee members — Nancy Pitcairn, Janet Raske and Diana Regan for their word processing and editing of *Sound Seasonings*.

A special thanks goes to Marianne and Jack Sann whose home with its lovely view of Long Island Sound was used as a study for the cover art.

Recognition is also due the American Spice Trade Association; National Gardening Association; and Vanilla Information Bureau for contributing information to the Herb Primer.

About Our League

It started in the parlor. Small groups of New York Junior League members who'd left the city for the suburbs of Westchester County gathered together for tea and cake. It was 1933. A nationwide bank panic gripped the country. President Roosevelt told Americans that "The only thing we have to fear is fear itself," and the ladies in the parlor got organized.

Their social gatherings took on social purpose as they sewed layettes and rolled bandages for New York hospitals and later the Child Welfare Clinic of New Rochelle. In 1941, now designated as the Eastern Westchester Unit of the Junior League of the City of New York, they established a Welfare Fund and a library for pediatric heart patients. Soon their volunteer efforts centered around wartime activities.

In 1949, one hundred members of the Junior Service Group of New Rochelle swelled their ranks, helping to staff the Unit's recently opened "Outgrown" Shop, forerunner to our Golden Shoestring. The following year, the Soundettes began rehearsing and by October when a Junior League charter was granted to the Unit, they really had something to sing about! This marked the beginning of the League which has through the years evolved to become our League, the Junior League of Westchester on the Sound, representing the seven Sound Shore communities of New Rochelle, Larchmont, Mamaroneck, Harrison, Rye, Rye Brook and Port Chester.

We are as diverse as the communities we serve. Our League continues because we grow along with our communities. As a group we seem to share a fondness for children, our own and those of others.

For over twenty years, our Junior League delighted and enlightened children with puppet troupes. The Lilliput Theatre and then the Merri Messengers presented original productions of nursery classics such as "Jack and the Beanstalk," "Peter Rabbit," and "Goldilocks and the Three Bears." Staged in schools, libraries and hospitals, the productions allayed the fears of pre-operative children and presented palatable lessons on nutrition. For many children it was their first experience of live theatre. It was also an opportunity for the Junior League to enrich the cultural life of our community.

Four-year-olds were the focus again in 1975 when we introduced Listen, Hear! to the preschools, day care centers and playgroups. Initially concentrating on hearing problems, the screening program expanded to include vision impairment. League volunteers trained at the Burke Rehabilitation Center and the Westchester Lighthouse for the Blind. On a budget of only $575, twenty-five volunteers tested and retested over 2000 children.

The Junior League works in cooperation with other community organizations to research needs and get projects done. In 1956, the

4

Westchester County Council of Social Agencies determined through interviews with doctors, teachers, police and clergy, that during the previous year 414 families in the Larchmont and Mamaroneck area could have been referred to a family service agency had one been available. Our League got busy, organizing and joining forces with a Citizens Committee in a cooperative informational and fundraising effort for Family Service. A League staffed Speakers Bureau educated civic groups about what a family counseling service does. League publicity activities targeted the newspaper and radio station. The family station wagon sported a bumpersticker and League offspring plastered posters.

On April 21, 1957, a local office of the Family Service of Westchester opened in Mamaroneck offering personal counseling and through community outreach, helped to create an atmosphere conducive to happy family life.

In the 1960's, during a time of racial and intergenerational strife, our Junior League built bridges. We established YES, the Youth Employment Service. Working closely with Port Chester's Carver Center, we staffed a tutorial program and funded the community center's "mortgage burning."

The 70's dawned and with it a growing awareness of the toll our planet Earth had taken. Tom Wolfe called it the "Me" decade but our League had another priority.

The L.I.F.E. (Local Involvement for the Environment) Center opened in 1971, highlighting our 20th anniversary. Pulling together the Sound Shore area's many and diverse environmental groups, the Junior League pooled information, education and talent, creating a well-equipped resource center for students, teachers and the community. A calendar of conservation activities, programs, speakers and a roster of volunteers continues to encourage citizens of all ages to take an active and responsible part in improving the quality of our environment.

Throughout the 1980's, we've renewed our commitment to the family. In 1981, the League formed a Substance Abuse Task Force and in 1983, to heighten public awareness of the problems inexorably linked with alcohol and driving, S.A.F.E. was implemented.

The Junior League sponsors Spring Harvest and Emergency Services, providing food and clothing to area needy; Safe Place, a haven for runaway and homeless youth until professional help arrives and a holiday gift drive for children with AIDS and their siblings. The Soundettes troupe to nursing homes, hospitals, adult homes for the handicapped and senior centers with their unique music therapy.

We enter the 90's convinced that for every human situation there is both the need and opportunity for volunteers.

With our special gifts of time and enthusiasm, we hope to make our towns and villages and even our world a better place to live.

$\mathcal{S}$OUND $\mathcal{S}$EASONINGS

CHAIRMEN

Janet McLean Buchbinder   Betsy Livingstone Steers

RECIPE EDITORS

Janet Cullinan Raske, *Chairman*

Patricia Neilson Bailey   Diana Doubek Regan

COMMITTEE

Kathy W. Baker   Margaret Manley Parchen
Julia J. Blanchard   Mary Gray Sachtjen
Terrie Ewbank Henry   Andrea Sporer Simon
Lucy M. Johanson   Nora Barrett Tulchin
Maryellen W. Johnston   Diane W. Williams
Lisa Foster Liss

MARKETING

Nancy Clary Pitcairn, *Chairman*

Anne Chapman Amato   Sheila A. Lahey

Sabrina S. Fox

STEERING COMMITTEE
1988 - 1989

Patricia Neilson Bailey   Mary Busteed Roe
Janet McLean Buchbinder   Shiranne Davis Simmons
Caryl Henderson Herson   Betsy Livingstone Steers

TABLE OF CONTENTS

INTRODUCTION

Welcome to the *Sound Seasonings* kitchen, where lovingly prepared meals have special character, thanks to the glorious aromas and flavors of herbs and spices. A dash of an herb or a sprinkling of a spice can transform a recipe from mediocre to memorable. Consider your all-time favorite. Maybe it's Grandma's apple pie, warm from the oven and sweetly scented with cinnamon, or Mom's famous beef soup, chock full of vegetables and savory herbs. Or perhaps you think of Aunt Rose's tantalizing pork roast, rubbed with garlic and thyme and cooked to golden perfection. Without the essence of fragrant herbs and spices, these dishes just wouldn't have the same appeal.

In this cookbook, the members of the Junior League of Westchester on the Sound share their own treasured family recipes. All are deliciously seasoned and are as diverse as the colorful communities that border the scenic Long Island Sound. A special feature is the old-fashioned herb primer, which offers practical advice on buying, storing, cooking and growing the most often used herbs and spices.

So come into the *Sound Seasonings* kitchen and sample the delectable recipes. You'll be doing more than making a tasty meal — you'll be creating a memory for you and your family to cherish forever.

HERB PRIMER

CONTENTS

Herb Primer: Part I

A TREASURY OF CULINARY HERBS & SPICES

This alphabetical listing explains the characteristics of the herbs and spices most often used in cooking.

ALLSPICE

Characteristics: This spice, made from the berries of a tropical tree, has a warm, sweet taste. It is sold dried, in whole and ground forms.
Uses: Most popular in baked goods, such as cakes and cookies, but also good in puddings, dips, sauces for seafood, meat or poultry, and in pickling spices.
Sound Seasoning **Tip:** Compatible spices include nutmeg, cinnamon and cloves.

ANISE OR ANISEED

Characteristics: The seeds from the anise plant have a sweet and spicy licorice flavor. They are available dried, in whole form.
Uses: Frequently used in baked goods, including the traditional German pfeffernusse cookies, anise is popular in Scandinavian, Greek, East Indian, Moroccan, Arabic and Hispanic cuisines. Combined with cinnamon and bay leaves, it is a delicious seasoning for pork, fish, duck and game.
Sound Seasoning **Tip:** If you don't have any anise on hand, you can substitute fennel seed or leaf.

ARROWROOT

Characteristics: This mild starch is a thickener for gravies, sauces and glazes. It comes from the root of the tropical plant arrowroot. It is sold in dried ground form.
Uses: Arrowroot is frequently used in plain biscuits, puddings and jellies.
Sound Seasoning **Tip:** Because it is easily digestible, arrowroot is often used in infant and toddler biscuits.

BASIL

Characteristics: Basil has a sweet flavor, with a suggestion of mint and clove. Sweet basil is the type most often used for cooking and is sold in fresh and dried forms. The fresh leaves can be chopped, minced or used whole in recipes. Other varieties of basil, each with a distinctive flavor, include lemon, anise, cinnamon, lettuce leaf, green ruffles, bush, purple ruffles and dark opal basil.
Uses: Most often used in Italian dishes, pesto, tomato sauce and pizza, but is also a traditional ingredient in other Mediterranean cuisines,

and in Thai cookery. Basil enhances the flavor of lamb, veal, fish, poultry, pasta, beans, tomatoes, and a wide variety of vegetables such as eggplant, squash, onions and peas. Olive oil, lemon, garlic, thyme, rosemary, sage and summer savory complement the flavor of basil.

Sound Seasoning **Tip:** Fresh basil can be stored in tightly sealed plastic bags in the refrigerator for a few days. To keep longer, put basil leaves in an airtight container and cover leaves with a layer of olive oil; seal the container and freeze. *Do not wash basil before storing, as water blackens the leaves!*

BAY

Characteristics: These aromatic green leaves have a spicy flavor and a recognizable aroma, which becomes stronger when they are shredded or crushed. They come from the bay tree, which grows in temperate climates, and are sold dried, in whole and ground forms.

Uses: The leaves can be added to soups, stews, marinades or sauces, and are a traditional component in a *bouquet garni.* Bay blends well with peppercorns, saffron, garlic, allspice, citrus, and prepared or dried mustards.

Sound Seasoning **Tip:** Always remove whole bay leaves from the dish before serving!

BEE BALM OR BERGAMOT

Characteristics: A member of the mint family, bee balm has colorful scarlet flowers and a citrus flavor. It is not generally sold commercially and must be cultivated in the garden.

Uses: Bee balm leaves can be used whole or chopped to add a tangy citrus taste to duck, pork, sausages and curries. Its fresh flowers can be added to salads or used as a colorful garnish.

Sound Seasoning **Tip:** Bee balm complements fruits such as strawberries, apples, oranges, tangerines and melons and combines well with mint.

BORAGE

Characteristics: Borage leaves, stems and flowers have a cucumber flavor. It is difficult to preserve the flavor and color of this plant when dried, so always use fresh. As it is not generally available commercially, borage must be garden grown.

Uses: The leaves can be eaten raw, or can be steamed or sautéed and served as a vegetable. Stems can be peeled, chopped and used raw or cooked. Toss borage flowers into salads or use as a garnish. In candied form, the flowers make lovely decorations for pastries and desserts. Compatible herbs include dill, mint and garlic.

Sound Seasoning **Tip:** Borage is not suitable for long-term storage, so do not attempt to freeze it or dry it!

BURDOCK
Characteristics: This fast-growing, weedlike plant has a mild flavor, somewhat reminiscent of potato and celery. Not likely to be available commercially, it must be cultivated in the garden.
Uses: The fresh root can be scrubbed and peeled, then steamed or sautéed. Tender young leaves can also be used raw in salads or can be steamed or sautéed and served as a vegetable. Burdock blends well with ginger and lemon juice.
Sound Seasoning **Tip:** Celery root can be subsituted for burdock root in recipes.

CAPERS
Characteristics: Capers are the unopened flower buds of the caper bush. They have a strong, aromatic, salty flavor, which develops only after pickling. They are always sold in a pickling liquid.
Uses: Used in sauces and relishes for flavor, and as a garnish. They are a common ingredient in fish or seafood dishes and can be added as seasoning to salads and stews. Classic uses include French *tartare, remoulade,* and *vinaigrette* recipes. Tarragon, garlic, olives and lemon all complement the flavor of capers.
Sound Seasoning **Tip:** Never let capers dry out. Always carefully remove them from the jar, so that there is enough liquid left behind to cover the remaining capers.

CARAWAY
Characteristics: Caraway seeds have a sharp, nutty flavor with a hint of dill and anise. They are sold dried, in whole form.
Uses: Best known as an ingredient in rye bread, caraway seeds are also valuable for seasoning stews, beef or pork dishes, cabbage, dumplings, goose and sausages.
Sound Seasoning **Tip:** Since caraway seeds become bitter during long and slow cooking, it is better to add whole or crushed seeds in the last twenty minutes of cooking.

CARDAMOM
Characteristics: This flavorful Indian spice, tastes a little like ginger. Cardamom has a strong spicy taste and a pleasant aroma, faintly reminiscent of eucalyptus. It is sold dried, in whole and ground forms.
Uses: Enhances both sweet and savory dishes and is a key ingredient in curry powder. It adds flavor to squash, sweet potatoes, duck, pork, meatballs, coffee and sweet pastries.
Sound Seasoning **Tip:** Compatible spices include cumin and coriander seed.

CELERY, CELERY SEED AND CELERIAC

Characteristics: Fresh celery comes in green and white varieties, with the green stalks having a sharper taste than the white ones. Dried celery flakes are also available. Celeriac is a type of strong-flavored celery with a root like a turnip. Dried whole or ground celery seed has a very sharp flavor. Celery salt, a commercially prepared mixture of celery seed and salt, has a milder taste.

Uses: Celery leaves, stalks, seeds, salt or celeriac impart crisp celery flavor to soups, stocks, stews and salads. The leaves or seeds are often combined with peppercorns and bay leaves in a *bouquet garni* to enhance the flavor of soups, stews and other long-cooking dishes. Whole seeds can be used to flavor pickles. Ground seeds season dressings, seafood and vegetables.

***Sound Seasoning* Tip:** Use celery seed and celeriac sparingly, as their flavor can be overpowering!

CHAMOMILE

Characteristics: Chamomile actually comes from two different plants, both with the same name, daisylike blossoms and sweet apple fragrance. German chamomile (also known as wild chamomile, sweet false chamomile, or mayweed) is a tall annual herb, while Roman chamomile, is a shorter perennial with a stronger fragrance. Most people prefer the taste of German chamomile, over the medicinal-tasting Roman chamomile. Its only commercial availability is as an ingredient in herbal teas, but it can be grown in the garden.

Uses: A soothing apple fragrance and flavor make it popular for brewing into tea. Chamomile petals can also be used in salads.

***Sound Seasoning* Tip:** Because its flowers contain pollen, chamomile may cause an allergic reaction. Be cautious about drinking chamomile tea if you have allergies.

CHERVIL OR GARDEN CHERVIL

Characteristics: A relative of parsley, chervil has lacy leaves and a delicate flavor with a slight bite of anise. Its aroma is also reminiscent of anise or licorice. It is sold fresh in green grocers, specialty markets and some supermarkets, and is also available in dried form.

Uses: Often used as a garnish and for seasoning soups and salads. Also an ingredient of the French *fines herbes*. It blends well with tarragon.

***Sound Seasoning* Tip:** Chervil is best when added to a recipe just before serving.

CHICORY

Characteristics: This weed has a strong, bitter flavor similar to that of a dandelion. Fresh greens are available commercially.

Uses: While its roots are a primary ingredient in coffee and can be added to other hot beverages, chicory is also used as a salad green or as a vegetable. The fresh leaves can be shredded, chopped or left whole and used raw in salads. Whole leaves can be steamed or sautéed as a vegetable. Onions, chives, olive oil and vinegar complement chicory's bitter taste.

Sound Seasoning **Tip:** Chicory cannot be stored long-term, so do not attempt to freeze it or dry it!

CHILI POWDER

Characteristics: Chili powder is actually a combination of various ground chili peppers and other herbs and spices, such as cumin and oregano. It is available in different strengths, from mild to hot.

Uses: It is often used to flavor Mexican, Southeast Asian and Indian foods. Chili powder is an essential ingredient in curry dishes.

Sound Seasoning **Tip:** You may subsitute ground red pepper for chili powder, but use sparingly, for red pepper is extremely hot.

CHIVES AND GARLIC CHIVES

Characteristics: A member of the onion family, chives have a mild, sweet onion flavor. Garlic chives have a stronger and more garlicky flavor. Chives are sold fresh and freeze-dried.

Uses: The slender fresh leaves can be minced and used as an ingredient as well as a garnish. Chives suit about every type of food except sweet desserts, and particularly enhance fish and creamed cheeses. They also blend well with shallots, marjoram and tarragon.

Sound Seasoning **Tip:** If you don't have chives on hand, you can subsitute the green part of a scallion.

CILANTRO OR CORIANDER

Characteristics: This pungent herb looks a little like parsley, but its taste is different and much stronger. It has a spicy, slightly musty flavor that changes the character of any dish. It is sold fresh in green grocers, specialty markets and some supermarkets, and is also available in dried form.

Uses: The leaves are most often used raw, generally chopped and sprinkled on a dish or mixed in at the end of cooking. It is popular in Southeast Asian, Chinese, Mexican, and East Indian cuisines.

Sound Seasoning **Tip:** Cilantro should be added sparingly to recipes, because it tends to overpower other flavors.

CINNAMON

Characteristics: Cinnamon comes from the bark of the tropical cinnamon tree. It has a fragrant slightly sweet spicy flavor. Cinnamon is sold dried, in ground and whole stick forms.

Uses: It is used in a variety of dishes, from meat to pumpkin pie, and

is vital to East Indian, Morroccan, Indonesian, Arabic, Iranian, Scandinavian, Mexican, Hungarian, Chinese and Greek cuisines. Whole cinnamon sticks are often used to spice hot drinks, especially mulled wine and punch. Cinnamon is a very popular baking spice.
***Sound Seasoning* Tip:** Vanilla, nutmeg, fennel, black pepper, ginger, clove and cardamom enhance the flavor of cinnamon.

CLARY
Characteristics: Clary has a strong balsam-like fragrance and a slightly bitter taste similar to that of sage. The plant must be cultivated in the garden, however the oil of clary is extracted and used commercially as a flavoring in baked goods, puddings, beverages, and candies.
Uses: The fresh or dried leaves can be used like sage. The flowers may be used as a garnish, and tea can be made from the dried leaves and flowers.
***Sound Seasoning* Tip:** Sage can be subsituted for clary.

CLOVES
Characteristics: Cloves are actually small dried buds from tropical trees. They have a sharp, wintergreen-like flavor and are sold dried, in whole and ground forms. Clear clove oil is also available commercially.
Uses: Whole cloves are poked into meats, vegetables and fruits such as hams, onions and baking apples. Ground cloves can be stirred into marinades, stews, cake batters, puddings, spiced teas and coffees and mulled beverages. Remove the pointed whole cloves before serving. Cloves go well with nutmeg, allspice and cinnamon.
***Sound Seasoning* Tip:** Use clear clove oil for light foods, as ground cloves are apt to discolor them.

CORIANDER SEED
Characteristics: This pale yellow spice has an unusual flavor, resembling a combination of citrus, sage, cumin and caraway. It is sold in ground and whole seed forms.
Uses: Widely used in spice mixtures and curry powders, and to add variety to marinades, salad dressings, cheese, eggs, chili sauce, guacamole and pickling brines. It is a subtle ingredient in cakes, breads and pastries, particularly gingerbread. Coriander seeds are popular in the cuisines of Greece, Southeast Asia, China, Mexico, East India, South America, Spain, Central America and Thailand.
***Sound Seasoning* Tip:** Did you know that in its fresh form, coriander is called cilantro? The lacy cilantro leaves can be used as a flavor enhancer or a garnish. See the cilantro listing in this treasury.

CUMIN
Characteristics: Pungent and powerful, cumin has a distinctive flavor and is an essential ingredient in curry and chili powders. It resembles caraway seed, but is lighter in color and is available ground as well as whole.
Uses: A popular spice in Middle Eastern, Mexican, Indian and North African cuisines, it blends well with coriander, parsley, mint, black and red peppers, paprika and curry powder.
Sound Seasoning **Tip:** For optimum flavor, use freshly ground cumin.

CURRY POWDER
Characteristics: A blend of spices, curry powder usually includes cumin, coriander, cloves, cinnamon, cardamom, red pepper, black pepper, fenugreek, ginger, mace, nutmeg, mustard seed and turmeric. It ranges in flavor from mild to hot.
Uses: Mostly used in curries and chilies.
Sound Seasoning **Tip:** Try your hand at your own homemade curry powder by combining the above ingredients in various amounts, depending upon the flavor and hotness you desire.

DANDELION
Characteristics: This pesty weed is also a flavorful herb. Young, tender dandelion leaves taste a lot like chicory, while older leaves can have a stronger flavor similar to spinach. The leaves and flowers may be found in specialty markets and in some supermarkets, but are probably more available in your own backyard.
Uses: Leaves are often used raw in salads or steamed or sautéed as a vegetable. The flowers can be minced and added to butters, spreads and herbed vinegars, and used as garnishes. Dandelion blends well with garlic, tarragon, chervil and salad burnet.
Sound Seasoning **Tip:** Chicory leaves can be substituted for dandelion leaves.

DILL
Characteristics: Delicate dill is available in two forms: dillweed, the feathery leaves from the plant, and dill seed. Dillweed leaves are sold fresh and dried. Dill seed is sold dried, in whole form.
Uses: Dill leaves usually flavor fish, vegetable dishes and salad dressings or appear as a garnish. Dill seed is most commonly used as a pickling spice or in long-cooking recipes.
Sound Seasoning **Tip:** To store dill up to six months, place whole stems in a freezer bag and freeze. When needed, simply snip off the desired amount and return the bag to the freezer.

FENNEL

Characteristics: Fennel looks a little like celery, but has a large, rounded stem and thin, feathery leaves. Its flavor is similar to that of anise and licorice. Sweet fennel and Florence fennel are most preferred for culinary purposes. Sweet fennel is sold in whole seed form, as well as fresh. Florence fennel is sold fresh.

Uses: Goes well with vegetable dips, cream sauces and grilled fish. The fresh leaves can be used in salads or as a garnish and the tender stems can be eaten raw like celery. The seeds are popular in sausages, desserts, breads, cakes, cookies and beverages.

***Sound Seasoning* Tip:** Anise can be substituted for both fennel seeds and stalks.

FENUGREEK

Characteristics: Fenugreek seeds have a nutty flavor that combines the taste of celery and maple. Fenugreek is not often found in supermarkets, but the dried seeds may be sold in whole and ground forms in Indian specialty markets. Fenugreek is also an ingredient in commercially prepared curry powders.

Uses: A common ingredient in Indian curries, as well as in Middle Eastern, Mediterranean, Pakistani and African cuisines. Ground or whole, the seeds complement meats, poultry and marinated vegetables.

***Sound Seasoning* Tip:** Use sparingly, because too much fenugreek can add a bitter taste to foods.

GARLIC

Characteristics: This powerful herb gives a pungent flavor to many foods. Consisting of several cloves, garlic is covered with a thin, papery coating which must be peeled before using. There are many varieties and the skin may be white, pink or mauve. Bulbs vary greatly in size, as do the number of cloves. Tiny and giant varieties are available. Garlic is sold fresh, as well as dried, in minced and powdered forms.

Uses: Used to flavor anything except desserts. For subtle flavor, a fresh garlic clove can be added whole to long-cooking foods, like sauces, soups or stews. A cut clove of garlic can be rubbed directly on foods before cooking to season roasts or breads. For stronger flavor, garlic cloves can be chopped or minced and added directly to the recipe. Garlic butter, oil, vinegar and mayonnaise are also popular.

***Sound Seasoning* Tip:** Smashing the garlic with the flat end of a knife will release the flavor so it can be added to long-cooking foods; it also helps peeling.

GINGER
Characteristics: Ginger has a snappy, sweet flavor which adds zest to many foods. It is sold fresh, dried (both in pieces and in ground form) and candied.
Uses: Popular in the cuisines of China, Japan, Southeast Asia, East India, the Caribbean and North Africa for beverages, salads, meats, poultry, fish and vegetables. Ginger adds sweetness to desserts such as puddings, cakes, breads and cookies. It is compatible with cinnamon, nutmeg, garlic, coriander, cumin, black pepper, red pepper and chives.
Sound Seasoning **Tip:** To store fresh ginger, wrap first in a paper towel, then tightly in plastic wrap; refrigerate. It will last for about a month.

HORSERADISH
Characteristics: Extremely pungent and guaranteed to clear the sinuses, horseradish root contains volatile oils similar to those in mustard and has a powerful, sharp mustard taste.
Uses: Generally used raw in recipes which contain vinegar and cream, such as dips, salad dressings or sauces. Best known for its use with roast or boiled beef, it is also delicious with sausages, fish, ham and eggs. It complements strong-tasting vegetables such as beets and is an important ingredient in Russian cooking.
Sound Seasoning **Tip:** As a condiment for meat, sausages and smoked fish, combine grated fresh horseradish with vinegar and mayonnaise.

LAVENDER
Characteristics: The graceful purple flowers from this scented garden shrub have a wonderful fragrance. Grow lavender in your garden or purchase the leaves and flowers in dried form.
Uses: The perfumed flowers and leaves are used in vinegars, jellies and jams, and sparingly in salads.
Sound Seasoning **Tip:** If you plan to grow lavender in your garden, choose English Lavender, the hardiest of the species.

LEMON BALM
Characteristics: This delicate herb has a lemony flavor with a slightly minty undertone. It's often grown in gardens for its lemon-like fragrance and is not usually sold commercially, except as an ingredient in herbal teas.
Uses: The fresh leaves can be used generously in cooking; the leaves and stems can be dried and used for tea. Toss whole or chopped fresh leaves into salads, sauces, and marinades for fish, poultry, and vegetables or use the leaves to impart a lemony flavor to jams, jellies, fruit juices, custards, fruit salads and other desserts. Lemon balm is an

herb which can be used generously.

Sound Seasoning **Tip:** As a substitute for lemon balm, you can use lemon verbena, but use about half the amount called for. Lemon thyme can be substituted in equal amounts.

LEMON VERBENA

Characteristics: The leaves and flowers of this woody shrub release a sweet and strong lemony fragrance when rubbed. You will have to grow it in your garden, as generally, its only commercial availability is in herbal teas.

Uses: The fresh or dried leaves add a touch of lemony flavor to fish, poultry, vegetable marinades, salad dressings, jams, puddings and beverages.

Sound Seasoning **Tip:** Lemon balm can be substituted, but you'll need to double the amount.

LOVAGE

Characteristics: Lovage looks, tastes and is used like celery. You can grow it in your garden or buy the dried stems in some specialty markets.

Uses: The leaves and stalks can be used fresh or dried in salads, vegetables, meat and fish dishes. The stems are especially good when added to soups and stocks, or when braised and marinated. The seeds are used whole or ground in pickling brines, cheese spreads, salads, salad dressings and sauces.

Sound Seasoning **Tip:** Lovage can be used interchangeably with celery.

MACE

Characteristics: This sweet-flavored spice comes from the outer covering of a pit found in the peach-like fruit from the nutmeg tree. This pit is also the source of the spice, nutmeg. The nutmeg kernel is beneath the bright red mace covering. Mace has a similar flavor to nutmeg, and is available in ground form.

Uses: Mostly used to spice cakes, cookies and other sweet desserts such as custards and puddings. It blends well with cinnamon, black and red pepper, parsley and cilantro.

Sound Seasoning **Tip:** Since mace is one of the most perishable spices, it is best kept refrigerated in a tightly sealed jar.

MARIGOLD OR CALENDULA

Characteristics: The slightly bitter petals of this vivid flower can be used fresh or dried to add color and flavor. Generally, its only commercial availability is in herbal teas.

Uses: Often used in salads and soups. The petals can also be used to make tea.

Sound Seasoning **Tip:** Marigold flowers are sometimes used as a substitute for saffron, as they have a similar flavor and impart the same vivid yellow color to foods.

MARJORAM
Characteristics: There are many varieties of marjoram, but sweet marjoram is most frequently used for cooking. It tastes like oregano, but is milder and sweeter. It is available dried, in whole or ground forms.
Uses: The leaves of flowers are used fresh or dried in cooking. The fresh sprigs are particularly flavorful in salads. Marjoram is good rubbed into roasts and great for flavoring tomatoes, pizza and spaghetti. It is often added to stews, sautés, marinades, dressings, herb butters, flavored vinegars and oils, cheese spreads, soups and stuffings. Compatible herbs include parsley, dill, nutmeg, cinnamon, bay leaves, garlic, onion, thyme and basil.
Sound Seasoning **Tip:** Marjoram can be used interchangeably in most recipes that call for oregano.

MINT
Characteristics: There are several different kinds of mint, each with its own distinctive, refreshing flavor. **Peppermint** is the strongest of the mints and is more frequently used commercially to flavor candies and sweets than it is for culinary purposes. **Spearmint** and **curly mint** are much milder than peppermint. **Apple mint** and the white-leaved **pineapple mint** have slightly fruity flavors. Mint leaves are available in fresh and dried forms and in extracts.
Uses: Peppermint can be used sparingly in the kitchen to enliven hot and cold beverages. **Spearmint** and **curly mint** enhance a variety of foods, including lamb, jelly, beans, salad greens, fruits, sauces, chocolate and tea. **Apple mint** and **pineapple mint** are beautiful garnishes and add zest to fruit salads or creamy cheeses.
Sound Seasoning **Tip:** When shopping for fresh mint, look for bright green, unblemished leaves and a fresh minty aroma.

MUSTARD
Characteristics: The two kinds of mustard seeds are valued for their hot, spicy flavor. White mustard seeds, which can be white or pale yellow, have a milder flavor and are frequently used in commercial bright yellow mustards. Black mustard seeds, which range from brownish to dark black in color, are stronger and are used to make French-style mustards or mustard powder. Mustard oil, frequently called for in Indian recipes, is sold in gourmet or Indian specialty stores. Many flavors of prepared mustards are also available.
Uses: Whole white mustard seeds can be used for pickling, in

preserving meats and fish and as a garnish on vegetable salads. Dry mustard powder gives excellent flavor to a variety of dishes. Prepared mustards enhance poultry, fish and many grilled recipes.

***Sound Seasoning* Tip:** Use mustard seed and mustard powder sparingly, as their flavor can be overpowering.

NASTURTIUM
Characteristics: The leaves and the reddish-orange petals from this flower have a peppery taste. They must usually be cultivated in the garden.

Uses: The leaves and flowers can be used fresh in salads, and the vibrant petals make a lovely garnish, particularly floating on the top of a fruity punch.

***Sound Seasoning* Tip:** Nasturtium vinegar can be made by soaking the flowers in a pint of vinegar for several weeks, then straining the vinegar and pouring it into decorative bottles.

NUTMEG
Characteristics: This sweet-flavored spice comes from the inner kernel found in the peach-like fruit from the nutmeg tree. (See **MACE**). Dried nutmeg is sold whole, for grating freshly into foods, and ground.

Uses: Can be used in many desserts, such as cookies, puddings, pies and cakes, and in creamy beverages such as eggnog. It especially complements cheese and spinach and is popular in meat and cheese dishes, such as ravioli.

***Sound Seasoning* Tip:** To keep the aroma fresh, store ground or grated nutmeg in the refrigerator. Whole nutmeg can be stored in a dark cool dry place.

ONION
Characteristics: Though commonly viewed as a vegetable, onion can also be considered an herb because of its distinctive flavor. Of the fresh varieties, white onions are the strongest; yellow ones are a bit milder, and red onions are the mildest and sweetest. Frozen onions are available in whole and chopped forms. Dried chopped onion, onion powder, flakes, and salt are also available.

Uses: Onions can be used raw, sautéed, steamed, broiled, boiled, baked, pickled, deep-fried in batter or carmelized. They add delicious flavor to many meat, cheese, soup, stew, dip, casserole, salad and vegetable recipes.

***Sound Seasoning* Tip:** Store fresh onions where air can circulate around them so they'll keep longer.

OREGANO
Characteristics: This sweetly flavored herb is a favorite ingredient in

Italian recipes. Both the fresh and dried leaves are used to flavor foods.
Uses: Oregano blends well with olive oil, and is frequently used to flavor tomatoes and cheese-based recipes such as pizza, tomato sauce and calzones. Oregano enhances egg and vegetable dishes, and seasons meat, poultry and fish. Compatible herbs and spices include garlic, thyme, parsley, cumin and cinnamon.
Sound Seasoning **Tip:** Marjoram can be used interchangeably in most recipes that call for oregano.

PAPRIKA
Characteristics: Paprika is a bright red spice with a mild, sweet flavor. It is sold in ground form.
Uses: Known as the national spice of Hungary, paprika is an essential spice for goulash, paprikas and many other Hungarian dishes. It is also delicious in grilled foods, marinades and egg dishes. It is frequently used to add color to eggs, chili and casseroles.
Sound Seasoning **Tip:** Paprika is mild and sweet enough to be used in generous quantities.

PARSLEY
Characteristics: The varieties of parsley most often used for cooking are the delicate curly parsley and the more robust flat leaf or Italian parsley. Parsley's gentle flavor goes well with almost any food.
Uses: In addition to being a garnish, parsley can be chopped and added to sautéed dishes, poultry, fish and grilled meats. Whole sprigs of parsley are often added to stocks and soups. Parsley is an essential ingredient in many herb and spice combinations, such as traditional *fines herbes* and *bouquets garnis*. Excellent in butter sauces, it complements the flavor of dill, oregano, thyme, garlic and pepper.
Sound Seasoning **Tip:** Chervil can be substituted for parsley.

PEPPER (BLACK, WHITE AND GREEN)
Characteristics: Black, white and green peppercorns all come from a tropical vine, which yields green berries that ripen to a bright red. **Black peppercorns** are harvested when green and then dried so they turn black. **White peppercorns** are allowed to ripen, then are hulled and dried. White pepper is milder than black pepper. Both are sold whole or ground. **Green peppercorns** are young, undried berries with a fresh, very strong flavor. They are sold whole, in freeze-dried form or packed in brine or vinegar.
Uses: Ground pepper enhances almost all dishes except desserts. Generally, white pepper is added to pale-colored foods and sauces where specks of black pepper would spoil the appearance. Whole peppercorns are added to pickles, marinades, soups or stocks, meat, poultry and fish.

Sound Seasoning **Tip:** Freshly ground pepper is preferable to pre-ground pepper in most recipes.

PEPPER, RED

Characteristics: The various kinds of red peppers available all come from a plant known as the capsicum or pepper plant. **Ground red pepper** or cayenne pepper is an extremely pungent type of ground red chili pepper. **Crushed red pepper** is also available. **Chili peppers** vary in shape and size, and can range in flavor from mild to very hot. You can purchase fresh green, red or orange chilies, as well as dried chilies. Chili powder is a blend of several varieties of ground chilies.

Uses: Ground or crushed red pepper will add firey flavor to many recipes, and even a dash of this spice adds a hot bite to foods. It is often used in native American, Cajun, Creole, Spanish, Mexican, Southeast Asian, Szechuan and East Indian recipes and is especially good with eggs, cheeses, creamy soups, sauces and curries. It is an essential ingredient in chili powder. **Chili peppers** are most often used in Mexican cooking, but are popular in other cuisines where hot food is favored, such as Thai, Indian and Chinese. Ground chili peppers are an essential ingredient in chili and curry dishes.

Sound Seasoning **Tip:** Red pepper and some of the hot chili peppers, such as jalapeños must be used sparingly.

POPPY SEED

Characteristics: These tiny blue-black seeds have a nutty flavor that complements a variety of foods. They are sold whole in jars or cans. White poppyseeds, popular in Indian cooking, can be found in stores specializing in Indian foods.

Uses: Whole poppy seeds are frequently used in baking and are often sprinkled on breads, rolls, cakes and pastries. Useful in herb butters and vinaigrette dressings, they add flavor to noodle and curry dishes. Toast or sauté the poppy seeds to enhance their flavor before adding them to any recipe which does not require cooking.

Sound Seasoning **Tip:** Poppy seeds spoil when not refrigerated. Store them in an airtight container in the refrigerator and they should last about six months.

ROSE, ROSEHIPS AND ROSE-PETALS

Characteristics: This fragrant, beautiful flower is also a tasty herb. Rosehips are the berry-like fruit of the rose plant and are tangy in flavor and rich in vitamin C. They are available dried or in tea blends and can be found in health food stores. Rose petals are sold fresh and candied, and as an ingredient in rose water.

Uses: The fragrant petals of the rose are popular as a garnish in salads

or fruit punches and are also used to make rose water, a favorite ingredient in East Indian and Arabic cuisines. Candied petals can be used in decorating cakes and pastries. Rosehips are used to make syrups, jellies, jams, conserves, teas, wines, soups and purées. They are also used in baked desserts such as pies, tarts, quick breads and muffins.
Sound Seasoning **Tip:** Roses most appropriate for the herb garden are the rugosa rose, the damask rose, the French rose, and the cabbage rose.

ROSEMARY
Characteristics: Rosemary's dark green leaves resemble pine needles, and even the flavor of this slightly minty herb is reminiscent of pine. Both the leaves and the flowers can be used for cooking and garnishing. Rosemary is sold fresh and dried.
Uses: Rosemary's strong flavor goes well with roasted or grilled lamb, poultry, fish, beef, pork and game. It also enhances many vegetable and egg dishes.
Sound Seasoning **Tip:** Compatible herbs include parsley, sage, thyme, garlic and oregano.

SAFFLOWER
Characteristics: The dried orange flowers from this annual plant can be used to add a rich red color to foods and can be found in some specialty stores. Safflower oil, a cooking oil valued for its cholesterol-reducing qualties, also comes from this plant.
Uses: Dried safflower adds color to soups, sauces, marinades, flavored vinegars and curries.
Sound Seasoning **Tip:** One-fifth the amount of saffron can be substituted. Keep in mind that safflower gives a reddish color, while saffron will yield more of a golden color.

SAFFRON
Characteristics: Saffron is contained in the orange-red stigmas of the crocus flower. To get just one pound of saffron, the stigmas have to be hand-picked from over 75,000 crocuses. Because of the high production costs, saffron is one of the most expensive spices on the market. Fortunately, only a dash of this sunny yellow spice is required to add bittersweet flavor and golden color to foods. Saffron is sold dried, in ground and whole-thread forms.
Uses: It is a favorite in stews, rice or fish recipes and is a traditional ingredient in French *bouillabaisse,* Spanish *paella,* and the cuisines of East India, the Middle East and North Africa. Saffron is sometimes an ingredient in cakes, breads, cookies, cheeses and eggs.
Sound Seasoning **Tip:** Though it's difficult to find a spice that can match saffron's flavor, there are a few spices that will give foods a

similar golden color. These include turmeric, dried marigold leaves or dried safflower leaves. When substituting, you'll need five times as much dried marigold leaves or safflower leaves.

SAGE
Characteristics: Sage has a pleasantly bitter taste, with a touch of lemon and a hint of camphor. Of the fresh varieties, garden sage is the most readily available, but flavored sages such as pineapple and clary sage can be grown in the garden, as can golden or dwarf sage. Sometimes available fresh, sage is also sold dried, in whole and ground forms.
Uses: Sage is best known for its use in stuffing on Thanksgiving, but is also a favorite in casseroles, sausage dishes, marinades, omelets, soups, breads and rolls. The leaves can be tossed into salads and vegetable dishes.
***Sound Seasoning* Tip:** Rosemary, thyme, parsley and garlic all enhance the flavor of sage.

SALAD BURNET
Characteristics: This bushy herb has a flavor that's similar to cucumber. Not generally available commercially, it must be grown in the garden.
Uses: The tender young leaves can be used as a garnish, in salads, flavored vinegars, herb butters and iced beverages. The seeds bring flavor to vinegars, marinades and cheese spreads and the pink flowers garnish salads and punches. Compatible herbs include dill, basil, thyme, garlic, oregano, marjoram and tarragon.
***Sound Seasoning* Tip:** Young borage leaves can be substituted in recipes that call for salad burnet.

SAVORY (SUMMER AND WINTER)
Characteristics: Summer savory is mildly peppery and tastes a little like thyme, while **winter savory** is stronger with a flavor reminiscent of pine. Both are available dried, but can be grown in the garden and used fresh.
Uses: Both types of savories are most popular in beans and salads, fish or smoked meats, patés, vegetables and flavored vinegars.
***Sound Seasoning* Tip:** Savory blends well with thyme, marjoram, oregano, rosemary, lavender, fennel or basil. You can make your own flavorful seasoning mixtures by adding dried savory to any combination of these dried herbs.

SCENTED GERANIUM
Characteristics: Scented geraniums are not really like the garden geraniums, although their leaves do resemble each other. Each variety of scented geraniums has its own characteristic fragrance. Most

preferred for cooking are rose, peppermint, lemon balm and lime geraniums. Scented geraniums must be grown in the garden.

Uses: The leaves from all except the peppermint variety will add distinctive flavor to cakes, puddings and jellies. Rose geranium leaves and peppermint geranium leaves add zip to tea.

***Sound Seasoning* Tip:** For a perfumed sweetener for flavoring desserts and hot beverages, place rose geranium leaves and granulated sugar in a glass jar. Let stand about two weeks in a sunny spot; then remove the leaves and the fragrant sugar is ready to use.

SESAME SEED

Characteristics: Sesame seeds have a pleasant nutty flavor which is enhanced by toasting or sautéing. Ground sesame seeds are known as sesame meal.

Uses: Sesame seeds are delicious on breads, rolls and biscuits, in salads and with cheeses. Frequently used in meat, fish and chicken dishes as an alternative to breadcrumbs, sesame seeds are also used as a garnish and replace nuts in many recipes. Ground sesame seed is made into a paste called tahini, a condiment that's very popular in Greek and Middle Eastern cuisines.

***Sound Seasoning* Tip:** To keep them their freshest, store sesame seeds in an airtight container in the refrigerator or freezer.

SORREL

Characteristics: Sorrel has a somewhat bitter leaf, similar to spinach in looks and taste. It may be found fresh in specialty stores or in the produce section of your market. No commercially dried sorrel exists.

Uses: The leaves can be steamed or cooked briefly and served as a vegetable or chopped and added raw to salads. They can also be cooked and puréed and served as an accompaniment to veal, pork, fish and eggs. Sorrel is particularly delicious in soups and blends well with parsley, chives, thyme, oregano and nutmeg.

***Sound Seasoning* Tip:** Use only the youngest, most tender leaves, as older sorrel leaves have a very bitter taste.

SWEET CICELY

Characteristics: This attractive, old-fashioned herb has a flavor that combines anise and celery. It must be grown in the garden.

Uses: The leaves are used in salads and as garnishes. Roots can be steamed and served as a vegetable and the seeds are used in candy, syrups, cakes and liqueurs. It goes well with strong vegetables such as cabbage, turnips, brussels sprouts and parsnips, and is wonderful in soups and sauces.

***Sound Seasoning* Tip:** Anise and caraway seeds can be substituted for Sweet Cicely.

TARRAGON

Characteristics: The leaves of this classic culinary herb have a strong flavor that's sweet and slightly bitter at the same time. Tarragon should be used sparingly and should be added to recipes in the final minutes. It is available fresh or dried.

Uses: One of the French *fines herbes*, tarragon can be added to salads and used as a garnish. A traditional ingredient in classic French recipes such as *remoulade*, tartar sauce, *bearnaise*, and French dressing, it complements many vegetables and most meats, fish and seafood. It is excellent in flavored vinegars, herbed mayonnaise or butter, and cream sauces. Chervil, parsley, oregano, thyme and garlic enhance tarragon.

***Sound Seasoning* Tip:** If you're planting tarragon in the garden, look for the French variety.

THYME

Characteristics: The delicate flavor of thyme goes well with almost any food. The leaves are available dried and can sometimes be found fresh. French thyme is the most common variety, but lemon thyme, English thyme, caraway thyme and oregano thyme are also good to plant in your garden.

Uses: One of the French *fines herbes*, thyme leaves and sprigs are used to garnish salads, and are favored in French, Cajun and Creole dishes cooked slowly in wine. An essential ingredient in *bouquet garnis*, it works well with all kinds of meats and fish, and is often added to stews, soups and stocks. Thyme is a favorite in herbed butters, mayonnaise, flavored vinegars, mustard and bean dishes. It blends well with garlic, basil, oregano, sage, pepper, parsley, dill, mint, marjoram and rosemary.

***Sound Seasoning* Tip:** Before adding thyme to recipes, crumble dried sprigs or chop fresh or frozen leaves to release the full flavor.

TURMERIC

Characteristics: Like ginger, this vivid yellow spice comes from an underground root. However, turmeric is sweeter and more fragrant than ginger, with a delicate, aromatic, slightly peppery taste. Turmeric is sold dried in ground form.

Uses: Turmeric is an essential ingredient in curry powders, adding flavor as well as bright yellow color to the dish. It is also frequently added to mustard powder, pickles and chutneys, deviled eggs, salad dressings and marinades. Complementary spices include curry powder, chili powder, cayenne pepper and black pepper.

***Sound Seasoning* Tip:** When used for adding color to foods, only a tiny amount is needed to create a brilliant yellow tone.

VIOLETS

Characteristics: The leaves and flowers of sweet, fragrant violets can be used to garnish salads, chilled soups and punches; the petals are often candied and used to decorate cakes, pastries and poached fruit. Candied violets and violet water are available commercially.

Uses: Violets add sweetness to jams, jellies, liqueurs, puddings, flans and gelatins. Violet water is used in tea, breads, cupcakes, puddings, ices, fruit compotes and chilled soups.

***Sound Seasoning* Tip:** To make your own violet water, steep the leaves and petals in boiling water for a few hours, or until the water is fragrant. Strain the water and use to flavor cold soups, fruit, beverages and desserts.

VANILLA

Characteristics: Mellow, aromatic vanilla is one of America's most popular flavors. It is available in dried whole bean and liquid extract forms.

Uses: Although it's most often used to flavor sweet desserts such as cookies, cakes, pies, puddings, ice creams and fruit dishes, vanilla enhances the flavor of many foods and can be used creatively in seafood, fish, poultry, veal and vegetable recipes.

***Sound Seasoning* Tip:** For the best flavor, make sure the vanilla beans, extract and vanilla-flavored products you purchase carry a label that states it is pure or "100% real vanilla." Artificially-flavored vanilla products are inferior in taste.

WATERCRESS

Characteristics: This peppery herb, rich in vitamins and minerals, is best known for its use as a salad green. Fresh watercress is available commercially. No dried watercress is sold.

Uses: In addition to adding piquant flavor to salads, watercress is delicious in sandwiches, creamed soups or bouillon, and can be steamed or boiled and served as a vegetable. It can also be chopped and added to other herbs such as parsley and chives to season a variety of dishes.

***Sound Seasoning* Tip:** Nasturtium flowers have a peppery flavor similar to watercress and can be substituted for it in salad recipes.

Herb Primer: Part II

KITCHEN WISDOM
Here's all you need to know about cooking with herbs and spices.

BUYING GUIDE

Fresh: When purchasing fresh herbs and spices, select those with vibrant colors, unblemished leaves or skins, and a strong fragrance.

Dried: Most dried herbs and spices must be purchased in sealed jars. However to judge the freshness of opened spices on your pantry shelf, the "sniff test" is invaluable. If the aroma of the spice is weak or you have to smell it more than once to pick up the scent, then it's time to replace it. Remember that whole spices like cinnamon sticks and cloves don't reveal their full fragrance until broken, heated or crushed. The color of the spice should be vibrant, not faded — particularly in the case of paprika or ground red pepper. Dried herbs should also have a bright, fresh color. It's helpful to add the purchase date to the jar.

HOW TO STORE

Fresh: Except for garlic and onions, which should be stored in a cool, dry, airy place, most fresh herbs and spices can be stored in the refrigerator. For sprigs, wash; shake off excess moisture and dry herbs thoroughly with paper towels; then store whole in tightly sealed glass jars or plastic bags in the refrigerator, where they'll keep for about a week. Do not wash basil before you store it, as water blackens the leaves. Bunches of herbs can be placed stem end down into jars which have been filled with a few inches of water; then covered with plastic wrap and refrigerated for about a week.

Dried: Most dried herbs and spices should be stored away from direct light and heat. Paprika, red pepper, chili powder, parsley flakes, poppy seeds and sesame seeds retain their flavor and color best when stored in the refrigerator.

ADVICE ON FREEZING HERBS

Herbs retain their freshness and flavor when frozen, and can be added to foods without thawing. However, since freezing destroys crispness, do not use frozen herbs as a garnish.

Freezing the Leaves Whole: Shake or brush off dirt, arrange whole leaves flat on a cookie sheet and freeze for several hours. Transfer the leaves to freezer bags, label, seal and return to freezer. Use whole or minced.

Freezing in Sprigs: Freeze herbs separately or in flavorful combinations by arranging the sprigs in airtight containers or freezer bags before labeling, sealing and placing in the freezer. Frozen sprigs can be used whole to add to soups or stews or snipped and minced as needed.

Freezing Minced Herbs: Measure minced herbs by the tablespoon and freeze in ice cube trays. When the herb cubes are set, transfer to an airtight container or plastic freezer bag and return to the freezer. Use as needed. You can also make herb pastes by adding a little oil to your minced herb mixture. Pour a tablespoon into ice cube trays; freeze until set; then transfer to an airtight container or plastic freezer bag and return to the freezer. Use as needed.

GADGETS FOR GRATING, GRINDING AND CRUSHING

Grating and Grinding: Whole herbs and spices can be grated or ground with a blender, food processor or electric spice grinder. Small hand graters are designed especially for spices such as nutmeg and allspice.
Crushing: A mortar and pestle or garlic press are best for crushing whole herbs and spices.

SUBSTITUTING DRIED FOR FRESH

Fresh and dried herbs can be used interchangeably in most recipes, but it's important to remember that dried herbs are much more potent than fresh ones. When substituting fresh for dried use about three times more fresh herbs than dried.

LOW-SODIUM SEASONING SUGGESTIONS

When eliminating salt from a recipe, increase the amount of herbs and spices in recipes by about 25% and double the marinating time for poultry and meat for more complete flavor penetration. With long-cooking dishes, reserve about 25% of the seasonings to add during the last ten minutes of cooking, and make sure the herbs are finely crushed before adding to the recipe.

At-A-Glance Seasoning Chart

Try these flavorful combinations for spicing up all kinds of foods.

For Poultry
- Rosemary and thyme
- Tarragon, marjoram, onion and garlic
- Cumin, bay leaf and saffron or turmeric
- Ginger, cinnamon and allspice
- Curry powder, thyme and onion

For Fish and Seafood
- Cumin and oregano
- Tarragon, thyme, parsley and garlic
- Thyme, fennel, saffron and red pepper
- Ginger, sesame seeds and white pepper
- Cilantro, parsley, cumin and garlic

For Beef
- Thyme, bay leaf and onion
- Ginger, dry mustard and garlic
- Dill, nutmeg and allspice
- Black pepper, bay leaf and cloves
- Chili powder, cinnamon and oregano

For Pork
- Caraway, red pepper and paprika
- Thyme, dry mustard and sage
- Oregano and bay leaf
- Anise, ginger and sesame seeds
- Tarragon, bay leaf and garlic

For Vegetables
- *Green Beans:* Marjoram and rosemary; caraway and dry mustard
- *Broccoli:* Ginger and garlic powder; sesame seeds and nutmeg
- *Cabbage:* Celery seeds and dill; curry powder and nutmeg
- *Carrots:* Cinnamon and nutmeg; ginger and onion
- *Corn:* Chili powder and cumin; dill and onion
- *Peas:* Anise and onion; rosemary and marjoram
- *Spinach:* Curry powder and ginger; nutmeg and garlic
- *Squash (summer):* Mint and parsley; tarragon and garlic
- *Squash (winter):* Cinnamon and nutmeg; allspice and red pepper
- *Tomatoes:* Basil and rosemary; cinnamon and ginger

For Potatoes, Rice and Pasta
- *Potatoes:* Dill, onion and parsley; caraway and onion; nutmeg and chives
- *Rice:* Chili powder and cumin; curry powder, ginger and coriander; cinnamon, cardamom and cloves
- *Pasta:* Basil, rosemary and parsley; cumin, turmeric and red pepper; oregano and thyme

For Fruits:
- *Apples:* Cinnamon, allspice and nutmeg; ginger and curry powder
- *Bananas:* Allspice and cinnamon; nutmeg and ginger
- *Peaches:* Coriander and mint; cinnamon and ginger
- *Oranges:* Cinnamon and cloves; poppy seeds and onion
- *Pears:* Ginger and cardamom; black or red pepper and cinnamon
- *Cranberries:* Allspice and coriander; cinnamon and dry mustard
- *Strawberries or Kiwi Fruit:* Cinnamon and ginger; black pepper and mustard

Classic Seasoning Blends

Apple Pie Spice: This commercial blend of ground sweet baking spices includes cloves, nutmeg or mace, allspice, and ginger, and is used in all kinds of fruit pastries and pies.

Barbecue Spice: To add zest to grilled recipes, make your own homemade blend of ground spices. A suggested combination: chili pepper, cumin, garlic, clove and paprika.

Bouquet Garnis: These homemade or purchased bundles of herbs and spices are used to flavor soups and stews. They are usually tied up in a tiny cheesecloth bag so flavors but not particles will be absorbed into the food. Remove when cooking is complete. An essential ingredient in French cooking, bouquet garnis traditionally contain parsley, thyme and bay. To make your own, tie a few fresh sprigs of parsley and thyme, along with a bay leaf in a square medical gauze pad and tie with white thread. Experiment with your own combinations.

Chili Powder: This pungent, commercial blend is made from dried chilies and a variety of herbs and spices.

Chinese Five Spice Powder: The five spices in this tasty blend are Szechuan peppercorns, cinnamon, cloves, fennel and star anise. Found in Chinese markets or specialty stores, it is used as a condiment or to season pork and fish.

Cinnamon Sugar: Keep a homemade mixture of sugar and cinnamon on hand to add to cereals, toast, desserts and other sweet treats. Available commercially.

Curry Powder: The basic seasoning in Indian cooking, curry powder is a combination of ground spices and may include coriander seed, cumin, nutmeg, mace, cardamom seed, turmeric, mustard seed, chilies, fenugreek, ginger, peppercorns, garlic, allspice, cinnamon, cayenne pepper and fennel seed. Available commercially, you can also make your own homemade version.

Fines Herbes: One of the classic French seasonings, this mixture combines chervil, parsley, thyme and tarragon. Add to recipes at the final stages of cooking. You can purchase fines herbes or use a homemade mixture.

Pickling Spice: This commercial blend is used for pickling and preserving meats or for seasoning vegetables, stews, soups, sauces and relishes.

Poultry Seasoning: For use primarily in poultry, this commercial blend of ground sage, thyme, marjoram, savory, and rosemary also adds flavor to pork, veal, beef and fish.

Pumpkin Pie Spice: In addition to being used in pumpkin pies, this commercial blend of ground cinnamon, nutmeg, clove and ginger is also wonderful in pastries and spice cookies.

Quatre epices: Quatre epices, which in French means four spices, is a spice blend for flavoring meats and sweets. The blend is usually a combination of any four of the following spices: cloves, mace, nutmeg, ginger, cinnamon, black pepper, or white pepper. Available commercially, you can also use a homemade mixture.

Vanilla Sugar: This flavorful homemade sweetener is used in desserts, hot beverages or cereals. Add a split vanilla bean to two cups of sugar, cover, and set aside for about six weeks before using.

VINEGARS, OILS AND OTHER HERBED TREATS

FLAVORED VINEGARS

Fresh and dried herbs and spices can add wonderful zip to any kind of vinegar. Choose a mild vinegar. Wine or rice vinegars are best with herbs and spices, while white vinegars are better with delicate flowers. To flavor one pint of vinegar use about ½ cup of chopped fresh herbs, a handful of fresh herb sprigs, or about 3 tablespoons of dried herbs or spices.
To Make: Heat the vinegar until almost boiling, and then pour the hot vinegar over the flavoring. Cover and let stand in a warm, dark place for two or three weeks; then strain the vinegar and pour into clean bottles.
Best Flavor Choices: Thyme and rosemary; fresh ginger; crushed garlic and lemon peel; nasturtium petals, peppercorns and shallots; rosemary; rose petals; violet and nasturtium petals or parsley, sage and shallots.

FLAVORED OILS

Fresh or dried herbs or spices can be added to any oil, but the best are olive, vegetable, safflower, sunflower or walnut oils. Add single herbs or combinations.
To Make: In a glass bottle, pour the oil over the flavorings, cover and store bottle in a warm place for a few weeks before using.
Best Flavor Choices: Rosemary; basil; tarragon; basil, oregano, thyme and parsley; oregano, thyme and garlic; rosemary, thyme, sage and marjoram; fresh ginger, cardamom seed and cilantro or chili

powder and crushed garlic.

HERB BUTTERS

Just a few tablespoons of herbs added to a cup of softened butter makes a savory spread. For breakfast breads and pastries, try combining butter with mint and dill or lemon verbena and grated orange peel. To season roasted meats and poultry and grilled foods, add one of these mixtures to butter: basil, oregano and thyme; marjoram and garlic or garlic, sesame seeds and chives.

HERBAL ICE CUBES

Combine water and fresh chopped herbs in an ice cube tray and freeze. The herbal ice cubes will add flavorful sparkle to punches and iced teas.
Best Flavor Choices: Mint; violet petals; rose petals; lemon verbena; scented geraniums.

HOT TIPS FOR USING HERBS

• To mince fresh herbs, snip with scissors or chop finely with a sharp knife.
• To dry fresh herbs from your garden, tie the stems of the sprigs together and hang them in a warm, dry place away from direct sunlight, such as an attic, for about two weeks. Store in an airtight container.
• Avoid combining two strong herbs when cooking or the flavors will compete, overpowering the food.
• When combining a delicate herb, such as chervil and a strong herb, such as tarragon, in the same dish, use a minimal amount of the stronger herb so that it doesn't mask the flavor of the other.
• When you double the amount of a recipe, do not double the amount of herbs or spices. Simply use just a little more than called for in the original recipe.
• Fresh herbs lose their flavor when cooked for long periods of time. Add them in the final moments of cooking.
• To release the full flavor of a fresh or dried herb, crumble or rub the leaves between your fingers before adding to a recipe.
• In uncooked foods, such as dressings or marinades, taste before serving to determine if you need to add more seasoning, since the full flavor of the herb or spice may not have been released.
• To flavor meats, poultry or fish, rub in the herbs or spices with your fingers.
• Handle fresh red peppers with care, as their oils can actually burn your skin and irritate your eyes. Always wear rubber gloves when cutting them, and make sure that you wash your hands well afterwards.

Herb Primer: Part III

GROWING GUIDE

Fresh herbs can always be within arm's reach when you grow your own. Herbs are simple to cultivate and easy to care for, whether you grow them in the garden or in containers on the patio, terrace or windowsill.

BASIC GUIDELINES

Annuals vs. Perennials: Annual herbs need to be planted anew every year, while perennials will come back again from season to season. You'll probably want to choose a combination of annuals and perennials for your herb garden. Most herbs can be started as small nursery plants, but some may need to be started from seed. A basic culinary herb garden should include basil, chives, dill, lemon balm, marjoram, oregano, parsley, mint, rosemary, sage, savory and thyme.
In the Garden: All that is needed for most herbs to flourish in the garden is a sunny spot with well-drained, friable or powdery soil. (For exceptions to this rule, see our "Garden Varieties" chart.)
On the Sill: Herbs can be grown in any kind of container, as long as it has holes in the bottom for drainage. Place them individually in small pots or tuck several herbs together in large tubs. Choose a soil that drains well (one recommended mixture combines equal portions of topsoil, perlite, composted cow manure and peat moss) and set your herbs in the sunniest spot you have. Most herbs need at least five hours of direct sunlight daily.

MADE FOR THE SHADE

Don't despair if you think your property isn't sunny enough for an herb garden. The following herbs will thrive in shady conditions: celery, chervil, chives, coriander, dill, fennel, mint, parsley, sorrel, sweet cicely and violets.

CONTAINER HERBS

These herbs adapt quite well to container gardening: basil, bay, chives, coriander, dill, lemon balm, mint, oregano, parsley, rosemary, sage, sweet cicely, tarragon and thyme.

Garden Varieties Chart

Here's a listing of some of the best herbs for planting in your garden, plus a guide to their botanical characteristics.

HERB	TYPE	HEIGHT	SOIL PREFERENCE	LIGHT PREFERENCE
Basil	annual	2 feet	moderately rich	full sun or partial shade
Bay	perennial, evergreen	up to 10 feet	average, well-drained	full sun or partial shade
Bee Balm or Bergamot	perennial	3 to 5 feet	moist, rich	full sun or partial shade
Borage	annual	2 to 3 feet	average, well-drained	full sun
Chamomile	German: annual Roman: perennial	German: 2-3 feet Roman: 10 inches	rich, slightly acidic	full sun or partial shade
Chives & Garlic Chives	perennial	12 to 18 inches	well-drained	full sun or partial shade
Cilantro	annual	3 to 4 feet	average, well-drained	full sun
Dill	annual	3 to 4 feet	average, well-drained	full sun
Fennel	annual	3 to 5 feet	average, well-drained	full sun
Horseradish	perennial	2 to 3 feet	cool, moist & well-drained	full sun
Lavender	perennial	1 to 3 feet	dry, sandy	full sun
Lemon Balm	perennial	1½ to 3 feet	rich, moist	partial shade or full sun
Lemon Verbena	perennial	5 to 10 feet	average, well-drained	full sun
Lovage	perennial	4 to 6 feet	moist, well-drained	full sun or partial shade
Marigold	annual	1 to 2 feet	rich	full sun
Marjoram	perennial	12 to 18 inches	light, rich	full sun; warm climate

continued on next page

Garden Varieties Chart *continued*

HERB	TYPE	HEIGHT	SOIL PREFERENCE	LIGHT PREFERENCE
Mint	perennial	1 to 3 feet	moist, well-drained	full sun or partial shade
Nasturtium	annual	18 inches to 6 feet, depending on variety	average, well-drained	full sun
Oregano	perennial	2 to 2½ feet	light, well-drained	full sun
Parsley	annual	1 to 1½ feet	rich, well-drained	full sun
Rosemary	perennial	2 to 3 feet, but up to 6 feet in warm climates	sandy, well-drained	full sun or partial shade
Sage	perennial	up to 2 feet	average, well-drained	full sun
Savory	Summer: annual Winter: perennial	Summer: 1½ feet Winter: 1 foot	Summer: rich, light Winter: average, well-drained	Summer: full sun Winter: full sun or partial shade
Scented Geraniums	perennial	2 to 4 feet	average, well-drained	full sun
Sweet Cicely	perennial	3 feet	moist, well-drained	partial shade
Tarragon	perennial	2 to 3 feet	average, well-drained	full sun; moderate climates
Thyme	perennial	8 to 12 inches	average, well-drained	full sun
Violets	perennial	up to 1 foot	moist, rich	full sun or partial shade

Herb Gardens to Visit

Visiting public herb gardens is an excellent way to learn to identify the characteristics of various herbs. Here are some local gardens, as well as some not-so-local ones that are certainly worth the trip.

The Bible Garden At The Cathedral Of St. John The Divine, 1047 Amsterdam Avenue • New York, NY 10025 • 212-316-7400

Located on the grounds of the cathedral, the Bible Garden showcases herbs mentioned in the Bible, along with other Biblical plants and trees.

The Bonnefont Cloister Herb Garden, The Cloisters (a branch of The Metropolitan Museum of Art) Fort Tryon Park • New York, NY 10040 • 212-923-3700

This herb garden contains more than 250 species of plants that were cultivated during the Middle Ages. All the plants are labeled and are generally grouped in beds according to their uses.

Boscobel Restoration, Route 9D • Garrison-on-Hudson, NY 10524 • 914-265-3638

This historic federal period mansion and estate features an extensive herb garden for strolling.

Brooklyn Botanic Garden, 1000 Washington Avenue • Brooklyn, NY 11225 • 718-622-4433

This botanic garden has formal and informal herb gardens, and features a Shakespeare garden with herbs and other plants from the author's time.

Caprilands Herb Farm, 534 Silver Street • Coventry, CT 06238 • 203-742-7244

Run by renowned herbalist and author Adela Grenier Simmons, this famous herb farm features an 18th century farmhouse and restored barn, and over 30 herb gardens containing more than 300 varieties of herbs. Some of the gardens are grouped according to color or fragrance, while others display specific herbs. All are visually appealing and a delight to the senses. Herb enthusiasts will enjoy the luncheons, lectures, educational programs, crafts demonstrations, garden tours and special holiday celebrations offered at Caprilands. Call for schedule.

Gilbertie's Herb Gardens, 7 Sylvan Lane • Westport, CT 06880 •
203-227-4175

A retail gardening center specializing in herbs, Gilbertie's offers
gardeners all types of herb products. Shoppers will get ideas and
inspiration for their own herb gardens from the attractive display
gardens.

**Kitchawan Research Center (a branch of the Brooklyn Botanic
Garden),** 712 Kitchawan Road (Route134) • Ossining, NY 10562 • 914-941-8886

In addition to wooded areas, meadows and a number of walking
trails, this 12-acre center for botanical research has an extensive public
herb garden. The center also offers a variety of educational programs.
Call for schedule.

The National Herb Garden, The U.S. National Arboretum • 3501 New York
Avenue, N.E. • Washington, DC 20002 • 202-399-5958

This garden features a number of specialty herb gardens, each
designed around a certain theme. You'll find herbs important to the
colonists in the Early American garden, for example, and herbs
favored by native American Indians in the American Indian garden.
Medicinal, culinary, and beverage gardens are featured, as well as a
formal knot garden and a fragrant rose garden exhibiting species of
roses dating back to the early 1800s.

The New York Botanical Garden, Bronx, NY 10458-5126 • 212-220-8700

Surrounded by a brick wall with elegant wrought iron gates, The
New York Botanical Garden's Herb Garden is filled with over 80
varieties of fragrant, flavorful herbs. The garden was designed by the
Herb Society of New York.

Rochester Museum & Science Center, 657 East Avenue • Rochester, NY
14603 • 716-271-4320

The museum's Garden of Fragrance contains over 100 herbs and 50
rose varieties. It is patterned after the "Sweet Gardens of Memory," a
garden planted by the first colonists. There are eight geometric herb
beds, laid out in the formal, simplistic Tudor and Stuart style. They
include culinary herbs, salad herbs, pot herbs and flowers used for
food, aromatic herbs, bitter and repellant herbs, monk's herbs used
since the sixth century, bee-attracting herbs, and medicinal and
magical herbs.

APPETIZERS & BEVERAGES

Herbal Country Dip

Chopped vegetables complete this appetizer.

Planning:
Chill overnight

Preparation Time:
10 minutes

Yield:
Approximately 2 to 3½ cups

1   16-ounce carton sour cream
1   cup mayonnaise
4 to 6 scallions, chopped
1½ tablespoons chopped fresh parsley
1½ teaspoons dried dill, more may be added for additional flavor (if using fresh dill use only 1 teaspoon)

1¼ teaspoons seasoned salt
¼   teaspoon curry powder (optional)
crudites or chips

- Mix all ingredients in a large bowl. Cover and refrigerate overnight.
- Serve with crudites or chips.

Note: Leftovers can be served on baked potatoes.

Artichoke Parmesan Dip

Just keep the ingredients on hand for last minute guests.

Preparation Time:
5 minutes

Cooking Time:
25 to 30 minutes

Yield:
Approximately 1 cup

1   14-ounce can artichoke hearts, drained and cut up
½   cup grated Parmesan cheese
½   cup mayonnaise

1   7-ounce package Italian salad dressing mix
crackers or bread squares

- Preheat oven to 350°.
- In a bowl, whisk all ingredients together thoroughly.
- Pour into an ovenproof dish or crock.
- Bake uncovered for 25 to 30 minutes. Dip will be bubbly. Serve warm with crackers or bread squares.

Holy Guacamole

Planning:
Better if made one hour before serving, but don't make too far in advance (avocados will discolor)

Preparation Time:
10 minutes

Yield:
Approximately 2 cups

Always a favorite.

2 or 3 ripe avocados (preferably small bumpy skinned Haas avocados instead of large California ones)
juice of one lemon
2   tablespoons sour cream

1   teaspoon cumin
salt and pepper to taste
⅛   teaspoon cayenne pepper (optional)
1   clove garlic, pressed
tortilla chips

- Skin avocados and mash pulp. Place all ingredients in blender.
- Blend until smooth. Serve with tortilla chips.

Tangy Vegetable Dip

Planning:
Refrigerate at least two hours before serving, but better if chilled overnight.

Preparation Time:
10 minutes

Yield:
Approximately 2 cups

Great with raw vegetables or cooked shrimp.

1½ cups mayonnaise
3   tablespoons minced onion
3   tablespoons honey
3   tablespoons ketchup

3   tablespoons lemon juice
3   tablespoons curry powder
3   drops hot pepper sauce

- Whisk all ingredients together thoroughly. (Perfect in the food processor.)
- Place in serving bowl, cover and refrigerate.

Hot Pepper Dip

---

*A must at any football party —
or bring heated for tailgating.*

Planning:
Can be prepared in advance—
transfer to a casserole dish
before adding cream cheese.
Refrigerate until needed, add
cream cheese and bake
covered for 30 minutes at 350°.

Preparation Time:
10 minutes

Cooking Time:
20 to 30 minutes

Yield:
6 servings

1½ cups chopped onion
¼ cup butter
4 medium ripe tomatoes,
seeded and diced into
small cubes
3 large hot cherry peppers,
minced

salt to taste
1 8-ounce package cream
cheese, cut into cubes
nacho chips

- Sauté onion in butter until soft. Add tomatoes, peppers and salt.
- Simmer uncovered for 10 minutes. Add cream cheese and heat until melted.
- Serve warm with nacho chips.

Planning:
Can be prepared ahead and reheated in microwave

Preparation Time:
10 minutes

Cooking Time:
20 minutes

Yield:
1½ cups

Hot Mushroom Dip

A surprise for mushroom lovers.

8 ounces fresh mushrooms, coarsely chopped	1 cup sour cream
½ cup chopped scallions	½ teaspoon salt
4 tablespoons butter or margarine	⅛ teaspoon pepper
2 tablespoons all-purpose flour	⅛ teaspoon paprika
1 tablespoon milk	dash hot pepper sauce
	wheat toast and thinly sliced bagels

- Sauté mushrooms and scallions in butter or margarine. Sprinkle with flour. Blend and brown lightly. Add milk and only ½ cup sour cream.

- Continue cooking and stirring over low heat until mushrooms are tender. Add seasonings and remaining sour cream. Heat slightly. (When reheating, place in ovenproof crock and cook uncovered at 300° for 20 to 30 minutes.)

- Serve with wheat toast or thinly sliced bagels.

Note: Any leftovers can be used with a sautéed chicken or veal — or top a broiled tomato!

Santa Fe Dip

Be careful! This dip is addictive.

Planning:
Can be prepared in advance

Preparation Time:
30 minutes

Yield:
8 to 10 servings

1   16-ounce can refried beans
2   ripe avocados
2   teaspoons lemon juice
salt and pepper to taste
1   8-ounce carton sour cream
½   cup mayonnaise
1   package taco seasoning mix

2   large ripe tomatoes, finely chopped
4 to 5 scallions, finely chopped
1   4-ounce can sliced black olives
1   12-ounce package sharp Cheddar cheese, grated
tortilla chips

- On a large platter, layer ingredients as follows:
  — refried beans
  — avocados mashed with lemon juice, salt and pepper
  — sour cream, mayonnaise, taco seasoning mix, mixed together
  — finely chopped tomatoes
  — 4 to 5 finely chopped scallions
  — sliced olives
  — grated Cheddar cheese
- Serve at room temperature or refrigerate to serve later. Bring to room temperature at serving time.

Planning:
Can be layered ahead of time

Preparation Time:
10 minutes

Cooking Time:
20 minutes

Yield:
8-10 servings

North of the Border Mexican Dip

You can't have enough

1 8-ounce package cream cheese, softened
1 15-ounce can chili with beans
2 4-ounce cans green chilies, drained and chopped

4 to 6 scallions, chopped
1 12-ounce brick sharp Cheddar cheese, grated
plain taco chips

- Preheat oven to 350°.
- Spread cream cheese on the bottom of a 9x13x2-inch baking and serving dish. Layer chili with beans over cream cheese.
- Add green chilies, scallions and grated cheese on top.
- Bake for 20 minutes.
- Serve warm with chips.

Note: Black olives or guacamole can be added.

Carmela's Caponata

A wonderful, unusual side dish. An authentic Italian selection.

Planning:
Soak eggplant for one hour before cooking. Chill after preparing.

Preparation Time:
40 minutes

Cooking Time:
20 minutes

Yield:
2 to 2½ cups

2	large eggplants	¼	cup capers
1	tablespoon salt	¼	cup raisins
4	tablespoons olive oil	¼	cup pine nuts (pignoli)
1	large Spanish onion	1	6-ounce can tomato paste
10	green olives (slivered and pitted)	1	tablespoon sugar
2 to 3 cups celery hearts and tender parts		2	tablespoons wine vinegar
		fresh Italian bread	

- Peel and cube eggplant. Place in salted water (1 tablespoon salt with enough water to cover eggplant) and soak for one hour.

- Remove eggplant from water and squeeze excess water from eggplant. Deep fry in large skillet to a golden brown using half of olive oil. Drain on paper towels and set aside.

- In another large frying pan, add remaining olive oil and then sauté onion; add olives, celery, capers, raisins and pine nuts. Cook until celery softens.

- Add can of tomato paste and simmer for 10 minutes. Add sugar and vinegar. Heat gently.

- Blend fried eggplant into mixture and simmer another 10 minutes.

- Refrigerate in glass bowl or canning jars. Will keep for 2 to 3 weeks.

Note: Serve chilled or at room temperature. Spread on sliced fresh Italian bread.

Planning:
Need to start spread two days
in advance

Preparation Time:
10 minutes — day one,

Chutney Spread

*A unique combination
that serves many*

...ges cream	6 scallions, chopped
...ed	4 ounces peanuts, finely
...on juice	chopped
1 teaspoon mayonnaise	1 cup finely chopped black
1½ teaspoons curry powder or	olives
to taste (optional)	2 large hard-cooked eggs,
5 ounces chutney (liquid	finely chopped
strained out)	½ cup shredded coconut

- Two days prior to serving, wrap plastic wrap around the interior of a cake pan or pie plate. In a bowl, mix the softened cream cheese with lemon juice, mayonnaise and curry powder. Place mixture in lined dish and refrigerate overnight.

- One day prior to serving, unmold the cheese mixture onto serving platter and spread onto top of cheese the following layers.
    — chutney
    — scallions
    — peanuts
    — olives
    — eggs
    — coconut
  Cover and refrigerate overnight.

- Serve at room temperature with crackers.

Easy Herb Cheese

This looks great in 6-ounce souffle cups garnished with fresh dill.

Planning:
Needs to be refrigerated for at least 2 hours prior to serving

Preparation Time:
15 minutes

Yield:
10 servings

2 **8-ounce packages cream cheese, softened**
1 **cup butter or margarine, softened**
1 **teaspoon pressed garlic**
1 **teaspoon dried dill weed**
½ **teaspoon dried thyme**
½ **teaspoon marjoram**
½ **teaspoon dried sweet basil**
1 **teaspoon dried oregano**
salt and pepper to taste
fresh dill (optional)

- Cream together cream cheese and butter or margarine.
- Add herbs and mix until well blended. (Can use a food processor fitted with a metal blade.)
- Cover and refrigerate for at least two hours.
- Serve on crackers or as a filling for celery or cherry tomatoes.
- Garnish with fresh dill.

Planning:
Chill at least four hours or overnight

Preparation Time:
30 minutes

Yield:
8 servings

Smoked Salmon Ball

No one will believe this is made from a can of salmon. The liquid smoke is the secret!

1   16-ounce can red salmon
1   8-ounce package cream cheese, softened
1   tablespoon lemon juice
2   teaspoons freshly minced onion
1   teaspoon white horseradish
¼   teaspoon salt
½   teaspoon liquid smoke
3   tablespoons chopped fresh parsley
¼   cup chopped pecans
      wheat crackers or rye rounds

- Drain salmon, remove bones and skin and then flake with fork.
- In a medium bowl, mix cream cheese with lemon juice, onion, horseradish, salt and liquid smoke. Add salmon to mixture.
- Form into ball and chill at least four hours or overnight.
- Prior to serving, mix parsley and pecans together on flat surface. Roll refrigerated ball in mixture. Serve with wheat crackers or rye rounds.

Shrimp Mousse

Great for a buffet supper or summer party

Planning:
Chill at least 3 hours prior to serving

Preparation Time:
30 minutes

Cooking Time:
5 minutes

Yield:
4 cups

1   **10½-ounce can condensed tomato soup, undiluted**
1   **envelope unflavored gelatin**
¼   **cup *cold* water**
1   **cup mayonnaise**
1   **8-ounce package cream cheese, softened**

½ **to 1 cup finely chopped celery**
½ **to 1 cup finely chopped onion**
1   **pound shrimp, cleaned, cooked and chopped**

- Heat soup to boiling. Remove from heat and add package of gelatin which has been mixed with cold water. Set aside to let mixture cool.

- Once cooled, mix with mayonnaise and cream cheese. Add celery, onion and cooked shrimp. Mix well and place into a mold that has been well greased with mayonnaise.

- Cover with plastic wrap and refrigerate for at least 3 hours.

- Unmold and serve with crackers or fresh bread pieces.

Planning:
Marinate for three hours or overnight

Preparation Time:
20 minutes

Yield:
8 servings

Artichoke and Shrimp Bowl

Serve in a silver bowl. An easy first course for any dinner party.

1   egg yolk
½   cup olive oil
¼   cup wine vinegar
1½ tablespoons Dijon mustard
1   10-ounce package frozen artichoke hearts, cooked and drained

1   shallot — chopped fine (or 2 tablespoons minced onion)
2   tablespoons finely chopped fresh parsley
2   tablespoons dried chives
1   pound medium shrimp, cooked and cleaned

- Using blender or food processor, place egg yolk in container and blend for 10 seconds (with hand beater, mix for 2 minutes). Add oil, vinegar and mustard to egg mixture. Mix until just creamy.

- Finely chop artichoke hearts. Place in a glass bowl. Add shallots, herbs, and shrimp. Pour dressing over top. Marinate for a few hours or overnight.

- Place in serving dish and serve chilled.

Prosciutto and Parmesan Palmiers

This is truly easy, but your guests will be so impressed.

Planning:
Refrigerate 30 minutes before cooking. Can be partially made ahead of time.

Preparation Time:
15 minutes

Cooking Time:
20 to 25 minutes

Yield:
Approximately 18 palmiers

1   frozen puff pastry, thawed (18 x 11 inches)
3   tablespoons honey or sweet mustard
4   ounces thinly sliced prosciutto

1   cup freshly grated Parmesan cheese
parchment paper
1   egg
2   teaspoons water

- Place pastry on work surface and spread honey or mustard over top. Arrange prosciutto evenly over mustard to cover pastry; sprinkle with cheese. Lightly press cheese into prosciutto with hands or rolling pin.

- Starting at one long end, roll up pastry like a jelly roll to middle of sheet, then roll up other side until both rolls meet. Refrigerate until firm (at least 30 minutes).

- Preheat oven to 350°. Using a serrated knife, cut the rolls crosswise into ½-inch slices (each slice will look like an '8'). Place slices on cookie sheet covered with parchment paper.

- In a small bowl, beat egg with water. Brush top of each palmier with egg wash. Bake for 20 to 25 minutes. Palmiers will be puffed and golden. Check while cooking; time can vary due to oven temperature.

- Serve warm or at room temperature.

Hot Cheese Puff

Preparation Time:
15 minutes

Cooking Time:
20 to 25 minutes

Yield:
Approximately 35 pieces

This is almost too simple and disappears quickly.

4	8-ounce packages refrigerated crescent rolls
1	7-ounce round Gouda cheese
1	teaspoon Dijon mustard
1	egg, beaten
⅓	cup sesame seeds

- Preheat oven to 375°.
- Smooth out perforations from two packages of crescent rolls. Press to a 6x8-inch square. Do the same with the other two packages.
- Place one square on an ungreased cookie sheet. Lay cheese in center and coat with mustard. Encase cheese with second square section and seal openings. Brush top of square with egg. Sprinkle seeds on top.
- Bake for 20 to 25 minutes. Cut into squares or triangles.

Herb Cheese Stuffed Mushrooms

Preparation Time:
25 minutes

Cooking Time:
30 minutes

Yield:
8 to 10 servings

Fantastic! Guaranteed — not one will be left!

2   8-ounce packages cream cheese, softened
1   1-ounce package ranch dressing party mix
¼   cup mayonnaise
2   tablespoons minced onion
1   tablespoon chopped fresh parsley
¼   cup grated Parmesan cheese
1½   pounds mushrooms, washed and stems removed
1   cup crushed herbed stuffing mix
8   tablespoons butter, melted

- Preheat oven to 350°.
- Mix cream cheese, party dip mix, mayonnaise, onion, parsley and Parmesan cheese in a food processor or blender.
- Stuff mushrooms with cheese mixture. Dip the top of filled mushrooms into crushed stuffing.
- Place mushrooms into a buttered baking dish (quiche dish works nicely or glass pie plate).
- Pour melted butter over the top of mushrooms.
- Bake for 30 minutes.

Caution: These come out of the oven very hot — so give them a moment to cool.

Preparation Time:
10 minutes

Cooking Time:
25 to 30 minutes

Yield:
20 small squares

Chili Cheese Squares

A nice and simple hot hors d'oeuvre

2   **4-ounce cans whole
     roasted green chili
     peppers**
1   **8-ounce package Cheddar
     cheese, grated**

4   **eggs
     salt and pepper to taste**

- Preheat oven to 350°.
- Drain the chili peppers, remove any seeds and cut into thin slices. Line an ungreased 8x8-inch pan with the slices and press the grated cheese evenly and *firmly* on top.
- Beat eggs with some salt and pepper. Pour over the cheese.
- Bake for 25 to 30 minutes. The top will be lightly browned.
- Once cooled, cut into small squares. Serve warm or at room temperature.

Tortilla Olé

Terrific to eat and so nice to be able to make a day ahead of time.

Planning:
Refrigerate overnight. Take out early to heat or bring to room temperature.

Preparation Time:
20 minutes

Cooking Time:
If you choose, can be heated slightly before serving for 10 to 15 minutes.

Yield:
10 to 12 servings

1   8-ounce package cream cheese, softened
1   6-ounce can pitted olives, well chopped
4 to 6 scallions, chopped
2   4-ounce cans green chilies, drained and chopped

dash hot pepper sauce
6 to 8 tortillas (can be found in dairy section with refrigerated rolls)

- Beat cream cheese. Add black olives, scallions, chilies and hot pepper sauce.
- Spread this mixture evenly over each tortilla and roll up jelly roll style. Refrigerate overnight.
- Remove from refrigerator. If heating is desired, preheat oven to 350° and warm slightly for 10 to 15 minutes. Slice each tortilla into ½-inch pieces. Place on platter and serve. Slices will resemble pinwheels. Can also be served at room temperature.

Planning:
Sausage mixture can be
made up to two days in
advance

Preparation Time:
30 minutes

Cooking Time:
20 minutes

Yield:
20 pieces

Mimi's Sausage Treats

*You'll be sorry if this is not served at
your next winter gathering.*

1	pound hot or sweet Italian sausage, bulk	1	teaspoon Worcestershire sauce
3	cups finely chopped fresh mushrooms	1	8-ounce package refrigerated crescent rolls
½	cup finely chopped minced onion	1	8-ounce package cream cheese, softened
1	clove garlic, pressed	1	cup grated Parmesan or Romano cheese
1	teaspoon lemon juice		

- Preheat oven to 350°.
- Brown sausage in frying pan, breaking in small pieces.
- Drain off fat and add chopped mushrooms, onion and garlic. Sauté until tender. Add lemon juice and Worcestershire sauce.
- Spread sheet of crescent rolls onto bottom and up sides of an ungreased jelly roll pan. Spread cream cheese on top of rolls and then top cheese with sausage mixture. Sprinkle Parmesan or Romano cheese over top of mixture.
- Bake, uncovered, for 20 minutes. The top should be nicely browned. Cool slightly and cut into squares.

Tip: The first two steps can be made up to two days in advance. Just refrigerate sausage mixture in a covered container. Prior to baking, layer ingredients and cook for five minutes longer.

Classic Cocktail Meatballs

A hearty choice for a dinner buffet.

Planning:
Can be made ahead

Preparation Time:
10 minutes — sauce
15 minutes — meatballs

Cooking Time:
15 minutes — sauce (must be made first)
30 minutes — meatballs

Yield:
40 small meatballs

SAUCE:

1 tablespoon cornstarch	½ cup chopped celery
⅓ cup cider vinegar (can substitute wine vinegar)	¼ large green pepper, chopped
¼ cup soy sauce	1 7-ounce can pineapple tidbits in juice
½ cup water	
2 tablespoons brown sugar	

- Mix cornstarch and vinegar in small saucepan. Whisk in soy sauce, water and sugar.

- Place over medium heat and stir frequently to keep cornstarch from becoming lumpy. Heat until sauce is clear brown and starts to thicken.

- Add celery, green pepper and pineapple. Continue to cook for 5 more minutes.

MEATBALLS:

1 pound ground beef	½ medium onion, minced
½ cup bread crumbs	½ clove garlic, minced
⅛ cup milk (or water)	¼ large green pepper, minced
1 egg, beaten	salt to taste
⅛ teaspoon pepper	
¾ teaspoon soy sauce	

- Blend all ingredients together in large bowl. Shape into small bite-size balls.

- Place in large pot and cover with sweet and sour sauce. Bring sauce to boil and simmer over medium heat for 30 minutes.

- Serve in chafing dish to keep warm.

grace huntley pugh ©

MAMARONECK TRAIN STATION

They catnap, dream and scheme. They read, play cards and work. They rarely converse. In them, John Updike and John Cheever recognized the prototype for the latter day "Everyman", "New Yorker" short stories and cartoons dissect and lampoon them--the commuters.

At the beginning of 1849, the year of the California Gold Rush, the New York, New Haven and Hartford opened its line which followed the shores of Long Island Sound. In a short time, trains were transporting not only freight but passengers from country villages like New Rochelle, Mamaroneck, Rye and Port Chester.

Shake the family trees of some of Westchester's oldest families and down will tumble the original commuters on the 5:15 out of Grand Central.

The Iron Horse opened the west and the suburbs of Westchester as thousands of New York families moved out into the "healthful" suburbs, building homes, businesses, houses of worship, schools--communities.

And our communities flourished. By the end of the Civil War, 44 boarded the train in Mamaroneck for jobs in New York. Today, 1,625 begin their work day at this Victorian era station with a cup of coffee and THE TIMES.

New Orleans Shrimp

Keep toothpicks and napkins on hand for this treat.

Planning:
Can be prepared ahead

Preparation Time:
15 minutes

Cooking Time:
15 to 20 minutes

Yield:
6 to 8 servings

1   **pound butter or margarine (can use some of both)**
¼   **cup Worcestershire sauce**
¼   **cup white Worcestershire sauce**
4   **tablespoons coarse ground black pepper**
1   **tablespoon hot pepper sauce**
1   **tablespoon salt**
1   **tablespoon rosemary (ground or leaves)**

3   **cloves garlic, minced**
⅓   **cup lemon juice**
2   **lemons, sliced**
5   **pounds raw shrimp, shelled and deveined (36 to a pound is a good size — do not get larger)**
fresh bread slices, for garnish
toothpicks and napkins

- Preheat oven to 400°.
- In a small saucepan gently heat all the ingredients, except the lemon slices and the shrimp, until slightly simmering.
- Place shrimp and lemon slices in a large ungreased baking dish (preferably an oven-proof cast iron frying pan). Pour sauce over top of lemon slices and shrimp.
- Bake uncovered for 15 to 20 minutes, stirring once or twice while baking, until shrimp turn pink. Be careful not to overcook.

Note: Delicious warm or cold. Recipe is easy to halve or double. Serve with fresh bread and toothpicks.

Uncle Louie's Wings Marinara

Preparation Time:
30 minutes

Cooking Time:
Wings, 20 to 25 minutes
Sauce, 25 minutes

Yield:
48 to 72 pieces

Courtesy of Jay Leno, a famous comedian originally from New Rochelle

24 to 36 chicken wings, tips removed and split in half
all-purpose flour, for dredging
⅓ cup safflower or peanut oil, for frying (optional)
2 tablespoons olive oil (more to taste)
garlic cloves, pressed or garlic powder, to taste

1 28-ounce can Italian plum tomatoes
2 teaspoons chopped fresh parsley
salt
2 teaspoons hot sauce (preferably Durkee's)

- Cook chicken wings by broiling or lightly flour them and deep fry in safflower or peanut oil.
- While wings are cooking, heat ⅛-inch of olive oil in a medium saucepan. Add pressed garlic or garlic powder to taste. Using a food processor, slightly process one can of whole plum tomatoes, then press through a sieve and cook in the olive oil. Add a few teaspoons of chopped parsley and salt to taste.
- Heat sauce until simmering and then cook over low flame for about 20 minutes. Add hot sauce. (Add more if you like spicier food and a tastier sauce.) A bit more garlic can be added at this point, if desired. Cook another 3 to 4 minutes.
- Toss chicken wings in a bowl with half of sauce. Serve remaining sauce on side for dipping wings.

"Rye" Wings

A welcomed change from "Buffalo" wings

Preparation Time:
15 minutes

Cooking Time:
30 to 35 minutes

Yield:
4 to 6 servings as an hors d'oeuvre or 2 servings as an entrée

2   **pounds chicken wings**
⅓   **cup mayonnaise**
2   **tablespoons cider vinegar**
¼   **cup Dijon mustard**
2   **cups fine fresh rye bread crumbs (use food processor or blender)**

2   **teaspoons caraway seeds**
4   **tablespoons butter or margarine, melted**

- Preheat oven to 450°.
- Cut off chicken wing tips and halve wings at joint.
- In a bowl, whisk together mayonnaise, vinegar and mustard. Add wings and coat well.
- In another bowl, mix together bread crumbs and caraway seeds. Coat wings with bread crumb mixture.
- Place coated wings in an ungreased roasting pan or jelly roll pan. Drizzle melted butter or margarine over top. Bake for 15 minutes. Turn wings over and bake for an additional 15 to 20 minutes. Wings should be golden brown.

Chicken Fingers With Plum Sauce

Planning:
Chicken needs to be marinated overnight.

Preparation Time:
35 minutes

Cooking Time:
30 to 35 minutes (chicken only)

Yield:
15 servings

*A wonderful hearty hors d'oeuvre
— a sure crowd pleaser
(also good for a picnic)*

8   **chicken cutlets, skinned and boned**
1½   **cups buttermilk**
2   **tablespoons Worcestershire sauce**
1   **teaspoon soy sauce**
1   **teaspoon paprika**

salt and pepper to taste
2   **cloves garlic, pressed**
2   **cups plain bread crumbs**
½   **cup sesame seeds**
½   **cup butter or margarine, melted (can use a combination of half of each)**

- Cut chicken into ½x3-inch strips. Combine buttermilk, Worcestershire sauce, soy sauce, paprika, salt, pepper, and garlic in large non-metal bowl. Add chicken pieces, cover and refrigerate overnight.
- Preheat oven to 350°.
- Drain chicken. Combine bread crumbs and sesame seeds in a large baking pan. Add chicken pieces and toss to coat.
- Butter two 13x9x2-inch baking pans. Spread chicken out evenly and brush on melted margarine.
- Bake until golden brown, about 30 to 35 minutes. Serve warm or at room temperature. Serve with Plum Sauce.

Plum Sauce

1   **18-ounce jar red plum jam (about 1½ cups)**
1½   **tablespoons Dijon style mustard**

1½   **tablespoons prepared horseradish**
1½   **tablespoons lemon juice**

- In a small saucepan combine all ingredients. Whisk to mix well.
- Warm over low heat just until jam melts, stirring constantly.
- Serve either at room temperature or chilled.

Mandarin Chicken Wings

Sweet and sour at its best

Planning:
Marinate at least 3 hours, but better if allowed to soak overnight.

Preparation Time:
10 minutes, night before

Cooking Time:
50 to 60 minutes

Yield:
Approximately 48 pieces

24 **chicken wings (approximately 2½ to 3½ pounds)**
1 **cup sugar**
1 **cup water**
1 **cup soy sauce**
1 **cup corn or safflower oil**
¼ **cup *unsweetened* pineapple juice**
1 **teaspoon garlic powder**
1 **teaspoon ground ginger**

- Cut off chicken wing tips and then cut each wing into two pieces.
- Mix together all ingredients except chicken to make marinade. In a non-metal bowl or baking dish, pour marinade over chicken to cover. Marinate at least 3 hours, but better if overnight.
- Preheat oven to 350°.
- Strain marinade from chicken. On ungreased jelly roll pan, place chicken wings in one layer to bake.
- Bake uncovered for 50 to 60 minutes. Then place under broiler for a few minutes for extra crunch.

Note: Serve warm with lots of napkins.

Variation: Use chicken pieces and place on the grill for a barbecue crowd-pleaser.

Planning:
Chill prior to serving

Preparation Time:
10 minutes

Yield:
24 punch cups

Charlotte's Sunshine Fruit Punch

A welcomed non-alcoholic choice for any gathering.

½ cup sugar
½ cup hot water
1 6-ounce can frozen orange juice concentrate
1 6-ounce can frozen lemonade concentrate
1 46-ounce can pineapple juice, chilled

1 quart diet or regular ginger ale, chilled
½ quart seltzer, chilled
1 large block of ice, size of bread loaf pan or small bundt pan
1 orange, sliced
10 strawberries, optional

- Using a large bowl or pitcher, dissolve sugar in water. Add orange juice concentrate and lemonade concentrate. Chill for several hours.
- At serving time, set up punch bowl. Mix in concentrate mixture, pineapple juice, ginger ale, seltzer and block of ice. Decorate with orange slices and strawberries.

Preparation Time:
5 minutes

Yield:
2 servings

Banana Cooler

A smooth and satisfying choice

2¼ cups chipped ice cubes
1 lime, juiced
2 teaspoons confectioners' sugar

5 tablespoons white rum
2 ripe medium bananas, cut into chunks

- Combine half the ice, lime juice, sugar, white rum and bananas in a blender. With the cover on, blend at high speed for one minute or until smooth.
- Add the remaining ice and blend 1 minute more.
- Serve in tall chilled glasses.

Note: Rum can be deleted for a non-alcoholic version.

Wassail

Preparation Time:
15 minutes

Yield:
24 servings

*The perfect
accompaniment
for any fall
gathering.*

1   gallon sweet cider
1   quart hot tea
¼   cup brown sugar
5   lemons, juiced
3   sticks cinnamon

1   tablespoon whole allspice
1   teaspoon whole cloves
nutmeg to taste
3   oranges, sliced

- Mix cider, tea, brown sugar, and lemon juice in a 6-quart pot.
- Place cinnamon, allspice, cloves and nutmeg in a cheesecloth sack. Place sack in mixture.
- Bring wassail to a boil, and simmer for 15 minutes.
- Garnish with orange slices and serve hot in mugs.

Note: Rum or whiskey may be added if desired.

Lemon and Lime Mist

Preparation Time:
5 minutes

Yield:
6 servings

Cool and refreshing on a summer day

½   cup fresh lemon juice
¼   cup fresh lime juice
⅔   cup granulated sugar

1½ to 2 cups chilled club soda
½   cup chopped ice

- In electric blender, combine juices, sugar, soda, and ice.
- Cover and blend at high speed for 1 minute.
- Pour into chilled glasses.

Preparation Time:
5 minutes

Yield:
6 servings

Peach Slush

*Peach season never
tasted better!*

4   peaches, cut into small
    pieces (leave skin on)
1   12-ounce plus 1 6-ounce
    can of pink lemonade
    concentrate
6   ounces of vodka (use
    6-ounce can from
    lemonade concentrate to
    measure)

ice cubes
1   liter club soda (33.8 fluid
    ounces)

- Place peaches, lemonade concentrate, vodka and ice cubes in a blender. Blend until well mixed.
- Place 2 ice cream scoops of mixture in each glass.
- Add club soda and mix.

Note: For a decorative touch, add a sprig of mint!

White Sangria

Make sure you have enough!

Planning:
Prepare 1 hour in advance

Preparation Time:
5 minutes

Yield:
8 servings

1   **750-ml bottle dry white wine**
½   **cup curacao**
¼   **cup sugar**
1   **orange, thinly sliced**

1   **lemon, thinly sliced**
1   **lime, thinly sliced**
4 or 5 strawberries, sliced
1   **10-ounce bottle club soda**
ice cubes

- Combine wine, curacao and sugar in a large pitcher. Stir until sugar is dissolved.
- Add sliced fruits. Cover and chill in refrigerator at least 1 hour.
- Just before serving, add soda and ice cubes.

Autumn Punch

A novel combination to dress up fresh cider

Planning:
Chill for 3 hours

Preparation Time:
5 minutes

Yield:
20 servings

2   **12-ounce cans apricot nectar**
1½ **cups orange juice**

¾   **cup lemon juice**
1½ **quarts fresh cider**
20 **maraschino cherries**

- Combine apricot nectar, orange juice, lemon juice and cider in a large pitcher.
- Refrigerate at least 3 hours until well chilled.
- Add cherries. Serve in punch cups.

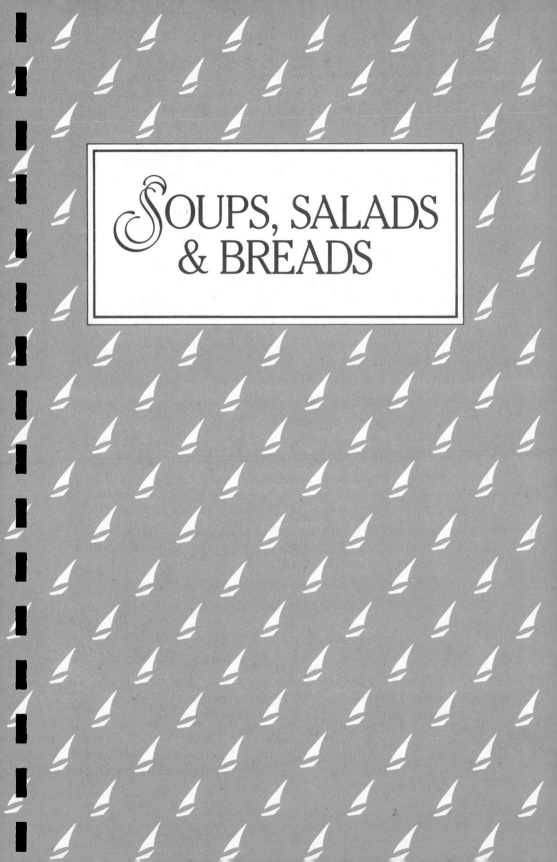

SOUPS, SALADS & BREADS

Versatile Vichyssoise

This is a lovely version of an all-time favorite chilled soup. But don't stop here. Look at the innovative variations that follow.

Planning:
Must serve chilled

Preparation Time:
20 to 30 minutes

Cooking time:
20 minutes

Chilling time:
At least 2 hours

Yield:
4 to 6 servings

2½ cups chopped leeks (about 3 large leeks)
2 tablespoons butter
1 pound potatoes (about 2 large)
3 cups well-seasoned chicken stock

1 cup light cream
salt and pepper to taste
¼ cup chopped chives for garnish
paprika for garnish

- When preparing the leeks, use only the white parts. Slice leeks vertically and separate into their layers. Wash well.
- Melt the butter in a large saucepan. Add leeks. Cover and cook until leeks are soft. Do not let the leeks brown.
- Peel and slice the potatoes. In another saucepan, combine the potatoes and the chicken stock. Cover and simmer the potatoes and stock until the potatoes are tender. Drain and reserve the stock.
- In a food processor or blender, purée the leeks and potatoes in batches while adding the chicken stock in a thin, steady stream. Cool the soup to room temperature.
- Add the light cream. Season to taste and chill for at least 2 hours.
- Garnish each bowl at serving time with a sprinkling of chives and paprika.

VARIATION I: *Artichoke Vichyssoise*

Ingredients for Versatile Vichyssoise (as listed above)

1 **9-ounce can artichoke hearts, drained**

- Prepare Versatile Vichyssoise recipe as listed above, except purée the canned artichoke hearts along with the leeks and potatoes.

VARIATION II: *Cucumber Vichyssoise*

Ingredients for Versatile
Vichyssoise recipe
EXCEPT reduce the light
cream to ⅓ cup

4 **cups purée of peeled and**
seeded cucumber
1 **teaspoon fresh dill weed**
(or ¼ teaspoon dried)

- Prepare Versatile Vichyssoise recipe, reducing light cream to ⅓ cup.
- Stir the purée of cucumber into the soup.
- Add the dill and serve.

Planning:
It may be refrigerated for
several days or frozen.

Preparation Time:
45 minutes

Cooking Time:
30 minutes

Yield:
8 to 10 servings

Spiced Tomato Bisque

Serve this well-seasoned soup year round. It
can be served hot or cold.

¼	pound butter	1	teaspoon marjoram
1	cup chopped celery	1	bay leaf
1	cup chopped onion	4	cups chicken stock
½	cup chopped carrots	1	pint heavy cream
⅓	cup flour	½	teaspoon paprika
2	1-pound 12-ounce cans whole tomatoes, drained and chopped	½	teaspoon curry powder
		¼	teaspoon white pepper
			salt to taste
2	teaspoons sugar		fresh parsley or fresh dill for
1	teaspoon dried basil		garnish

- Melt butter in a large saucepan. Sauté celery, onions and carrots until tender. Stir in flour. Cook 2 minutes, stirring constantly.
- Add tomatoes, sugar, basil, marjoram, bay leaf and chicken stock. Cover and simmer 30 minutes, stirring occasionally.
- Discard bay leaf.
- Purée ⅓ of the mixture at a time in blender.
- Add cream, paprika, curry, pepper and salt. Stir to blend.
- Serve hot or cold, garnished with fresh parsley or dill.

Chilled Curried Carrot Soup

Light and pretty. Nice for a summertime lunch at home, the beach or take along on a day of sailing.

Planning:
Must be prepared at least 5 hours in advance to allow for chilling time.

Preparation Time:
45 minutes

Cooking Time:
4 hours

Yield:
6 servings

¼ cup butter
1 large onion, chopped
1 pound carrots, pared and sliced
¾ teaspoon curry powder
1 thin strip lemon peel
2 cups homemade chicken stock (may use 1 13¾-ounce can chicken broth)

salt to taste
¼ teaspoon pepper
1 cup light cream or half and half
sprigs of fresh dill, coriander or parsley for garnish

- Melt butter in a large saucepan. Sauté onion and carrots until onion is tender (about 5 minutes). Add curry powder and lemon peel; cook 3 minutes.

- Pour chicken stock into a 1-quart measure and add water to make 1 quart. Add to onion and carrots. Bring to a boil; lower heat, cover and simmer about 20 minutes or until carrots are tender. Remove from heat and cool.

- Pour soup about one cup at a time into blender or food processor and blend until smooth. Pour blended soup into a large bowl. Add salt, pepper and cream. Stir.

- Cover and chill at least 4 hours before serving. Garnish with sprigs of fresh dill, coriander or parsley.

Planning:
Should be served
immediately

Preparation Time:
10 minutes

Cooking Time:
10 minutes

Yield:
4 servings

Spinach Stracciatella

An excellent soup to start an Italian meal.

2 **cups fresh spinach leaves,**
finely shredded
2 **tablespoons olive oil**
4 **cups well-seasoned**
chicken broth

2 **eggs**
1 **tablespoon cold water**
3 **tablespoons grated**
Parmesan cheese

- In a 2-quart saucepan, sauté spinach in oil until wilted (about a minute or two).
- Add the chicken broth to the saucepan and simmer 5 minutes.
- Beat eggs with water in a separate bowl. Slowly pour egg mixture into simmering soup, stirring constantly with a fork.
- Lower heat, taste for seasoning and serve at once with Parmesan cheese sprinkled on top of each serving.

Summer's Bounty Vegetable Chowder

A creamy soup loaded with vegetables of a summer harvest, but you will appreciate it anytime.

Planning:
Should be served immediately.

Preparation Time:
15 minutes

Cooking Time:
40 minutes

Yield:
6 to 8 servings

2	cups chopped celery	1	teaspoon salt
2	cups cooked corn (about 4 ears of fresh corn)	$\frac{1}{8}$	teaspoon pepper
1	medium onion, chopped	4	tablespoons butter or margarine
2	tablespoons diced green pepper	3	tablespoons flour
2	cups stewed, canned tomatoes	2	cups milk, scalded
2	cups cold water	$\frac{1}{2}$	cup grated cheese (Cheddar or Swiss, depending on preference)

- In a soup pot or large saucepan, combine celery, corn, onion, green pepper, tomatoes, water, salt and pepper. Heat to boiling and simmer for 30 minutes.

- While the vegetables are cooking, melt butter or margarine in a separate saucepan. Blend in the flour and cook, stirring for a few minutes. Gradually add the scalded milk to the flour and butter mixture, stirring constantly. Heat to boiling and cook for 5 minutes.

- Add the white sauce to the vegetable mixture. Add the cheese. Heat soup through while stirring occasionally until the cheese is melted. Serve immediately.

Planning:
Can be made ahead

Preparation Time:
20 minutes

Cooking Time:
30 minutes

Yield:
4 to 6 servings

Mushroom and Scallion Bisque

Subtle but savory.

1	bunch scallions	4	cups chicken stock
4	tablespoons butter	1	cup light cream
12	ounces mushrooms		salt and white pepper to taste
	(washed and sliced)		fresh chopped parsley for
4	tablespoons flour		garnish

- Peel scallions. Chop scallions including 2 or 3 inches of green tops.

- In a large saucepan, melt butter and sauté the scallions for a few minutes. Add 8 ounces of mushrooms and sauté the mushrooms and scallions just until soft but not brown.

- Blend the flour into the sautéed vegetables. Cook stirring for 1 minute.

- Remove the saucepan from the heat and slowly add the chicken stock, stirring well. Return the pan to low heat. Stir constantly while bringing the soup to a boil. Simmer for 20 minutes. The soup will thicken during the cooking process.

- Put the soup in blender or food processor. Add some of the remaining raw mushrooms, reserving a few for garnish. Blend the soup and raw mushrooms briefly. Return the soup to the saucepan.

- Add light cream. Reheat and add salt and pepper to taste.

- Soup may be served at once OR kept warm in a double boiler OR refrigerated until needed. At serving time, garnish with parsley and reserved raw mushrooms.

Creamy Cheddar Cauliflower Soup

A great flavor combination

Planning:
May be prepared in advance

Preparation Time:
20 minutes

Cooking Time:
20 minutes

Yield:
4 to 6 servings

1   head cauliflower, separated into flowerets
3   chicken bouillon cubes
¼   cup butter
1   small onion, chopped
2   tablespoons flour
2   cups light cream
1   teaspoon Worcestershire sauce
½   teaspoon salt
1   cup grated sharp Cheddar cheese (2 cups for richer flavor)
additional Cheddar cheese, paprika and chopped fresh parsley for garnish

- Simmer cauliflower about 15 minutes in water to cover (at least 3½ cups). Drain, reserving 3 cups liquid. Dissolve bouillon cubes in reserved water.

- Melt butter in a large saucepan. Stir in onions and cook until soft. Add flour and stir well.

- Gradually add the bouillon made from the cauliflower water to the onions. Slowly stir in the cream. Add Worcestershire sauce and salt.

- Add cauliflower and bring the soup to a boil. Remove from heat and stir in the cheese. Keep stirring until the cheese is melted.

- Ladle into individual bowls. Garnish with additional cheese, paprika and chopped fresh parsley. Serve hot.

Old Fashioned Mushroom Soup

Planning:
May be made ahead

Preparation Time:
20 minutes

Cooking Time:
1 hour, 10 minutes

Yield:
6 servings

Everyone will enjoy this simple soup. It is delicious with a bread and cheese platter.

6 tablespoons butter or margarine
1 pound fresh mushrooms, sliced
2 cups chopped carrots
2 cups chopped celery
1 cup chopped onion
1 garlic clove, pressed

2 10½-ounce cans beef broth
3 broth cans of water
4 sprigs fresh parsley
¼ teaspoon salt
3 tablespoons dry sherry or red wine
3 teaspoons tomato paste

- In a large soup pot, melt the butter or margarine. Add the sliced mushrooms and sauté for 5 minutes.
- Add carrots, celery and onion. Sauté for an additional 5 minutes.
- Add the remaining ingredients, bring to a boil and reduce the heat. Cover and simmer for 1 hour.

Note: It's easy to slice mushrooms quickly if you use an egg slicer.

This soup will keep in the refrigerator for a few days.

Lentil Pumpkin Soup

This recipe was made famous in Larchmont when served from hollowed-out pumpkins! It is a truly pleasing soup.

Planning:
May be frozen

Preparation Time:
10 minutes

Cooking Time:
40 minutes

Yield:
8 to 10 servings

2	cups chopped onions	⅛	teaspoon dried marjoram, crushed
¼	cup butter or margarine		
5	cups chicken broth	⅛	teaspoon dried thyme, crushed
1	16-ounce can pumpkin		
½	cup dry lentils		dash of hot pepper sauce
½	teaspoon salt	1	cup light cream
¼	teaspoon pepper		fresh parsley for garnish

- In a Dutch oven, cook onion in butter until soft.
- Stir in chicken broth, pumpkin, lentils, salt, pepper, marjoram, thyme, and hot pepper sauce. Cover and simmer for 35 to 40 minutes or until the lentils are tender. Let mixture cool slightly.
- Purée ⅓ of the mixture at a time in blender or food processor. (Soup may be frozen at this point. Add cream when reheating at serving time.)
- Return the soup to the Dutch oven and stir in the cream.
- Heat through gently. Garnish with parsley when serving.

Nantucket Autumn Soup

Preparation Time:
25 minutes

Cooking Time:
45 minutes

Yield:
8 to 10 servings

Make a meal of this soup

8   slices bacon, cut into 1-inch squares
4   onions, chopped
3   stalks celery, chopped
1   red pepper, diced
3   pounds potatoes, peeled and diced
3   cups fish stock or clam juice
½   teaspoon dried thyme
5   sprigs fresh parsley
2   cups milk
½   cup heavy cream
hot pepper sauce

freshly ground pepper
2   pounds cod, haddock or monkfish fillets, cut in large cubes
1¼   cups chopped, peeled tomatoes, or one 16-ounce can tomatoes, drained and broken up
½   pound scallops (bay or sea), cut into 3 pieces each
pats of butter and paprika or cayenne pepper for garnish

- Brown bacon in a large stock pot, stirring frequently. Drain on paper towels. Reserve 3 tablespoons of bacon fat.
- Add the onions, celery and red pepper to the reserved bacon fat in the stock pot. Cover and cook over medium/low heat until soft, about 10 minutes.
- Add potatoes, fish stock or clam juice and any additional stock or water required to cover vegetables. Bring to a boil. Put thyme and parsley in a cheesecloth bag for a bouquet garni. Add to soup. Reduce heat to simmer and cook until potatoes are tender (about 15 to 20 minutes).
- Purée half of the vegetables in a blender or food processor and return to the pot.
- Add milk, cream, a few drops of hot pepper sauce and freshly ground pepper to taste. Bring to a boil while stirring. Thin with more milk if desired.
- Add the haddock, cod or monkfish. Cover and cook for 2 to 3 minutes. Remove bouquet garni.
- Add tomatoes, scallops and bacon. Stir gently, cover and simmer until fish and scallops are just cooked through (about 1 or 2 minutes).
- Serve topped with a pat of butter and a sprinkle of cayenne pepper or paprika.

Leek and Clam Chowder

*New England clam chowder
with a continental touch*

Planning:
Better if prepared a day in
advance and refrigerated

Preparation Time:
10 to 15 minutes

Cooking Time:
30 minutes

Yield:
6 to 8 servings

1	bunch leeks, cleaned and chopped	4	cups milk
4	tablespoons butter or margarine	3	potatoes, peeled and diced
1	10-ounce can whole baby clams with juice (large can)	1	pint light cream
			salt and pepper to taste

- In a large saucepan or soup pot, cook the leeks in the butter over medium heat until they are limp.
- Add the clams and their juice. Add the milk and the potatoes. Cook the soup until the potatoes are tender (about 20 minutes).
- Add the cream. Refrigerate if serving later. Season with salt and pepper.
- Reheat gently at serving time.

Preparation Time:
25 minutes

Cooking Time:
30 minutes

Yield:
6 servings

Dutch Potato Soup

A satisfying soup with the smoky taste of bacon

4	cups potatoes, peeled and cut into ½-inch cubes	⅛	teaspoon pepper
3	cups water	6	slices bacon, diced
1½	teaspoons salt	1	medium onion, chopped
¼	teaspoon dried thyme leaves	2	tablespoons flour
		1	cup milk

- In a 3-quart saucepan over high heat, bring potatoes, water, salt, thyme and pepper to a boil. Reduce heat to low. Cover and simmer 15 minutes or until potatoes are tender.

- Meanwhile, in a 10-inch skillet over medium-high heat, cook bacon until browned. Drain on paper towels. Reserve 2 tablespoons bacon drippings.

- Drain potatoes, reserving broth. Mash half of the potatoes. Set aside broth, potatoes and mashed potatoes. Wipe saucepan dry.

- In same saucepan over medium heat, heat reserved bacon drippings until hot. Add onion. Cook until tender. Stir in flour until well blended.

- Gradually stir in reserved broth until smooth. Stir in mashed potatoes until smooth. Add bacon and cubed potatoes. Cook, stirring constantly, until soup is slightly thickened. Stir in milk. Cook until heated through.

Winter Soup

*No one will guess that you
didn't spend hours
simmering this soup.*

Planning:
Will keep for a few days in
the refrigerator

Preparation Time:
25 minutes

Cooking Time:
45 minutes

Yield:
8 servings

3 medium onions, chopped
2 tablespoons butter
1 pound ground beef
1 clove garlic, minced
3 cups beef stock
1 28-ounce can tomatoes,
  packed in purée
1 cup chopped carrots
1 cup chopped potatoes
1 cup chopped celery
1 16-ounce can green beans,
  drained

1 cup dry red wine
2 tablespoons chopped
  parsley
½ teaspoon bay leaf
½ teaspoon dried ground
  thyme
salt to taste
1 teaspoon pepper
Parmesan cheese, freshly
  grated, for garnish

- Sauté onions in butter until transparent.
- Add ground beef and garlic and sauté until beef is browned. Drain.
- Add all the remaining ingredients except the Parmesan cheese (garnish). Simmer until the vegetables are cooked or about 30 minutes.
- Serve with a sprinkling of Parmesan cheese over soup.

Potato Sausage Chowder

Preparation Time:
30 minutes

Cooking Time:
20 minutes

Yield:
8 servings

Men love this soup. It is hearty, tasty and a natural choice for a meal after a day of skiing or sledding.

3 tablespoons butter	1 pound favorite Kielbasa or Italian sausage (hot or sweet)
3 cups chopped onions (about 3 large)	
4 cups unpeeled, diced and scrubbed potatoes	2 cups milk
2 cups beef broth	½ teaspoon basil
	pepper to taste

- Melt the butter in a Dutch oven. Add onions and cook until soft, about 3 minutes.
- Add the potatoes and broth. Bring to a boil, cover, reduce heat and simmer 15 minutes.
- While the potatoes are cooking, slice the sausages into bite size pieces. Cook in a skillet until browned and cooked through. Drain.
- Add the sausage to the cooked chowder. Add milk and basil. Season to taste with pepper.
- Heat through to serve.

Golden Harvest Soup

Preparation Time:
10 minutes

Cooking Time:
6 to 8 minutes

Yield:
6 servings

This soup is reminiscent of all good things about autumn: fall foliage, apple picking, pumpkin carving...

2 12-ounce packages frozen puréed winter (butternut) squash, defrosted
2 tablespoons unsalted butter
1 cup unsweetened applesauce
1 cup light or heavy cream

¼ cup toasted walnuts, ground
2 teaspoons dried chervil, crumbled
½ teaspoon ground mace
salt and pepper to taste
½ cup toasted walnut pieces for garnish

- Combine all the ingredients except walnut pieces in a large saucepan and stir to blend well.
- Cook the soup over medium heat until warmed through (about 6 to 8 minutes).
- Ladle the soup into bowls and add a few chopped walnut pieces in the center.

Note: Keep ingredients on hand for an impromptu lunch.

grace huntley pugh ©

THE DUCK POND

It's a nice place to raise a family. The air is fresh, it rains a lot, and predators are few. So, each spring, year after year, the Northeastern brown mallard returns to the Duck Pond behind the Harrison Avenue Elementary School. An above ground, man-made water table, the pond is replenished by rains and an underground stream. From the air, it looks like a giant's tear drop.

The transient mallards join the four or five dozen year-round mallard residents, twelve Old White English ducks, and a Full Egret from South America who arrives in late March and is Rio-bound by Columbus Day.

They are spoiled rotten by the children of Harrison who feed the ducks an estimated 200 pounds of bread each week. For the children, many of whom begin their Duck Pond visits in a backpack or a stroller, it is often their first brush with nature. And for the ducks, despite a family of snappish turtles and occasional weasel raids, it's a good life.

Soundly Seasoned Vinaigrette

Preparation Time:
5 minutes

Yield:
1 cup

This dressing and its variations all have distinct personalities and serving ideas. The basic dressing is thick and tasty. It can be served with salads or steamed vegetables.

BASIC RECIPE:

½   cup olive oil
¼   cup Dijon mustard (smooth or coarse, depending on desired consistency)

2½   tablespoons balsamic vinegar
¼   teaspoon salt (or to taste)
5   grinds of pepper mill

- Whisk ingredients together until thick and smooth.

VARIATION 1: *Blue Cheese Vinaigrette*
- Add in ¼ cup crumbled blue cheese to the Basic Recipe. Do not overmix.

VARIATION II: *Parmesan Vinaigrette Dressing*
- Mix ¼ cup of grated Parmesan cheese into the Basic Recipe.
- Serve with Romaine lettuce and croutons.

VARIATION III: *Slightly Sweet Vinaigrette*
- Add 2 teaspoons of sugar to the Basic Recipe. Combine well.
- Serve with tomatoes and mozzarella. Simply slice tomatoes and mozzarella ¼-inch thick. Layer in concentric circles. Sprinkle chopped basil over tomatoes and mozzarella. Place a handful of Greek or Nicoise olives over all. Pour vinaigrette over all before serving.

VARIATION IV: *Poppy Seed Vinaigrette*
- Add 2 teaspoons sugar and 1 teaspoon of poppy seeds to the Basic Recipe. Combine well.
- Serve with a combination of lettuces such as Romaine, watercress, arugula, red leaf and endive. To this or a similar combination, add at least a sprinkling of raspberries for an unusual but delicious flavor contrast.

Note: Store unused dressings in the refrigerator for up to 2 weeks.

Planning:
Dressing should be put on salad 5 minutes before serving

Preparation Time:
10 minutes

Yield:
4 to 6 servings

Strawberry Almondine Spinach Salad

Wonderful summer salad. Very pretty.

SALAD:
½   pound spinach
1   pint strawberries

2   ounces toasted almonds

DRESSING:
½   cup sugar
2   tablespoons sesame seeds
1   tablespoon poppy seeds
1½ teaspoons minced onion
1¼ teaspoons Worcestershire sauce

¼   teaspoon paprika
¼   cup cider vinegar
½   cup vegetable oil

- Wash spinach and strawberries. Hull and slice strawberries.
- Tear spinach into bite-sized pieces and put in a salad bowl. Add strawberries and almonds to the salad bowl.
- Put all the dressing ingredients into a blender and blend for 20 to 30 seconds.
- Pour dressing over the salad 5 minutes before serving.

Green Beans with Creamy Tarragon Dressing

Planning:
Prepare at least 2½ hours before serving

Preparation Time:
10 minutes

Cooking Time:
5 to 10 minutes

Yield:
10 servings

This salad is creamy and tangy. It will add a lot to a barbecue.

---

3 **pounds green beans**
½ **cup mayonnaise**
⅓ **cup tarragon vinegar**
1¼ **teaspoons salt**
1 **teaspoon prepared mustard**

½ **teaspoon pepper**
1 **medium red onion, thinly sliced**

- About 2½ hours before serving or early in the day, put 1-inch of water in a 4-quart saucepan and bring to a boil. Add green beans and return to a boil. Reduce heat to low; cover and simmer 5 to 10 minutes until beans are tender but still crisp. Drain.

- In 13x9-inch baking dish, mix mayonnaise, vinegar, salt, mustard and pepper. Add green beans and onion; toss to coat well with the dressing.

- Cover and refrigerate at least 2 hours to blend flavors, stirring occasionally.

Goat Cheese and Herb Salad

Beautiful presentation

Planning:
Must be started 1 or 2 days in advance.

Preparation Time:
30 minutes

Cooking Time:
7 minutes, divided

Yield:
4 servings

½ pound very fresh goat cheese
1½ cups virgin olive oil
2 sprigs fresh rosemary
2 sprigs fresh thyme
4 large garlic cloves, smashed
1 teaspoon grated lime rind
fresh summer savory (optional)
fresh basil (optional)

½ pound baby vegetables (whatever you like best)
2 tablespoons olive oil
1⅓ tablespoons shallots, divided
salt and pepper
3 ounces sun-dried tomatoes
2 tablespoons sherry vinegar
2 heads Boston lettuce

- One or two days before serving, marinate goat cheese in olive oil, rosemary, thyme, garlic, lime rind and other herbs. Marinade should cover the cheese. Do not refrigerate.

- At least an hour before serving, clean vegetables. Leaving most of the vegetables whole, slice remaining vegetables to be about the same size. Sauté over low heat in a little olive oil, ½ teaspoon shallots, salt and pepper for about 5 minutes. Set aside and allow to cool.

- Cut tomatoes in strips and sauté over low heat in olive oil, ½ teaspoon shallots, salt and pepper for about 2 minutes. Set aside until serving time.

- Make vinaigrette by letting 1 tablespoon shallots soak in vinegar for about 5 minutes. Then whisk in some of the olive oil marinade, just to cut the vinegar's acidity. Add some of the herbs from the marinade and salt and pepper.

- To assemble, arrange Boston lettuce like a large flower on a plate. Then arrange baby vegetables with goat cheese in center. Finally add tomatoes on top and drizzle vinaigrette over all. Serve immediately.

Avocado Mango Salad

A colorful, interesting combination

Planning:
Dressing can be prepared in advance, but salad should be prepared just at serving time.

Preparation Time:
10 minutes

Yield:
6 servings

DRESSING:

¼ cup olive oil
2 tablespoons lemon juice

1 teaspoon Dijon mustard
1 tablespoon heavy cream

SALAD:

3 slices bacon, chopped
2 avocados, peeled and sliced
2 mangoes, peeled and sliced

½ cup walnut or pecan halves
lettuce (preferably red and green leaf lettuce)

DRESSING:

- Combine all ingredients in a screw top jar or salad dressing cruet. Shake well.

SALAD:

- Cook bacon in a skillet or in a microwave until crisp; drain.
- Arrange avocado, mango, nut halves and bacon over a bed of lettuce.
- Top with dressing and serve.

Planning:
Must be made 2 hours in advance

Preparation Time:
30 minutes

Cooking Time:
7 to 8 minutes

Yield:
8 servings

Prima Pasta Salad

The colors of this salad are striking.

1 teaspoon salt	1 small red pepper, seeded and cut in cubes
1 tablespoon vegetable oil	
2 cups uncooked corkscrew pasta (8 ounces)	6 medium mushrooms, washed and sliced
½ cup olive oil	4 ounces provolone or mozzarella cheese, cubed
¼ cup lemon juice, freshly squeezed	
½ teaspoon salt	1 9-ounce can chick peas (garbanzo beans)
¼ teaspoon freshly ground black pepper	⅓ cup pitted and sliced ripe olives (or more to taste)
pinch of cayenne pepper	1 6-ounce jar artichoke hearts, drained and quartered
1 garlic clove, crushed	
1 tablespoon fresh basil, snipped (or 1 teaspoon dry)	
1 small green pepper, seeded and cut in cubes	2 tablespoons chopped fresh parsley

- Bring 3 quarts of water, salt and vegetable oil to a boil. Add pasta, return to a boil and cook 7 or 8 minutes. Drain well, but do not rinse.

- While the pasta is cooking, combine ½ cup olive oil, lemon juice, salt, black and cayenne peppers, garlic and basil in a food processor or blender. Process briefly.

- Place the cooked, drained pasta (still warm) in a large bowl. Pour the dressing over the pasta and cool, unrefrigerated to room temperature.

- Add all the remaining ingredients. Toss lightly.

- Refrigerate covered for at least 1 hour. At serving time, retoss the salad.

Note: Pasta in a mix of colors is nice.

Birgit's Spring Harvest Salad

A Nicoise-style salad with a difference

Planning:
May be made an hour ahead, but add dressing at serving time.

Preparation Time:
20 minutes

Yield:
6 to 8 servings

1 pound green beans
1 large head loose leaf lettuce
1 pint cherry tomatoes, cut in half
1 6-ounce jar marinated artichoke hearts, drained
2 whole roasted red peppers (bottled or fresh), cut in strips
1 cup sliced pickled beets, drained
⅓ cup pine nuts, roasted
1 12½-ounce can solid white tuna, drained and flaked

DRESSING:
⅓ cup extra virgin olive oil
2 tablespoons balsamic vinegar
1 tablespoon Dijon mustard

- Cut green beans in half and steam until tender yet still crisp.
- Blend dressing ingredients together.
- Arrange a bed of loose leaf lettuce in a large salad bowl.
- Place all other ingredients in the bowl.
- Pour the dressing over all and toss.

Note: This salad is beautiful to present before tossing. Arrange the ingredients decoratively in the bowl. Pour the dressing on at the table and toss just before serving.

New Potato Salad with Pesto Dressing

Preparation Time:
30 minutes

Cooking Time:
10 to 15 minutes to cook potatoes

Yield:
6 servings

An old favorite with a new dressing

---

1 **pound small new potatoes**	1 **cucumber, peeled and sliced**
2 **tablespoons pine nuts (pignoli)**	**fresh basil leaves for garnish**

DRESSING:

1 **cup basil leaves, loosely packed**	2 **tablespoons grated Parmesan cheese**
2 **garlic cloves, crushed**	½ **cup mayonnaise**
2 **tablespoons pine nuts (pignoli)**	¼ **cup sour cream**

- Preheat oven to 350°.
- Boil or steam new potatoes until tender. Drain and place in salad bowl.
- While potatoes are cooking, place pine nuts, including those for the dressing, on a baking sheet. Toast for 5 minutes. Watch carefully, being sure that nuts reach a golden brown.
- Add the 2 tablespoons pine nuts and cucumber slices to the potatoes.
- Prepare the dressing and pour over the potatoes. Toss lightly and garnish with extra basil leaves.

DRESSING:

- Combine basil, garlic, the remaining toasted pine nuts and Parmesan cheese in a food processor. Process until smooth.
- Add the mayonnaise and sour cream. Process until well mixed.

Rice Twice Salad

Excellent main course luncheon fare

Planning:
Prepare at least 1½ hours before serving

Preparation Time:
20 minutes

Cooking Time:
40 minutes

Yield:
8 servings

½ cup wild rice
water
4 scallions, sliced
¾ pound mushrooms, sliced
4 tablespoons salad oil, divided
salt
½ cup regular long-grain rice
¾ pound oven-roasted boneless turkey breast
¾ pound cooked ham
¾ pound seedless green grapes

¼ cup red wine vinegar
2 tablespoons prepared mustard
1¼ teaspoons sugar
½ teaspoon dried thyme leaves
¼ teaspoon coarsely ground black pepper
salt to taste
¾ cup slivered blanched almonds, toasted
2 medium avocados

- One and a half hours before serving, or up to 1 day ahead, wash and drain wild rice. In a 2-quart saucepan over high heat, bring 1 cup water to a boil. Stir in wild rice. Reduce heat to low, cover and simmer 40 minutes or until rice is tender and liquid is absorbed. Remove saucepan from heat. Cool slightly.

- While wild rice is cooking, cook scallions and mushrooms in 2 tablespoons salad oil over medium-high heat in a 4-quart saucepan. Stir frequently during the cooking process. When the scallions and mushrooms are tender and lightly browned, add regular long-grain rice and 1 cup water. Heat to a boil over high heat. Reduce heat to low, cover and simmer 20 minutes or until rice is tender and liquid is all absorbed. Remove saucepan from heat. Cool slightly.

- Slice turkey and ham into long thin strips. If desired, cut each grape in half.

- In a large salad bowl, mix vinegar, mustard, sugar, thyme, pepper, remaining 2 tablespoons salad oil, and salt (to taste). Add
(continued)

wild and white rice, turkey, ham, grapes and toasted nuts to dressing mixture in bowl. Toss to coat salad with dressing.

- Serve salad at room temperature. If desired, cover and refrigerate to serve chilled later. To serve cut avocado in thin wedges. Arrange salad and avocado wedges on platter.

Note: Salad may be served at room temperature or cold.

Recipe may be doubled for large groups.

Purchasing thinly sliced turkey and ham from the delicatessen eases preparation of this salad.

Chicken Salad with Walnuts

Planning:
Must be prepared at least an hour in advance and up to 24 hours ahead.

Preparation Time:
10 to 15 minutes

Yield:
4 to 5 servings

Chicken with a crunch!

3 cups skinless, boneless cooked chicken, cut into bite-sized cubes	1 cup mayonnaise
½ cup finely chopped scallions	¼ cup coarsely grated fresh Parmesan cheese
½ cup broken walnuts	lettuce greens for serving
⅓ cup loosely packed, coarsely chopped, fresh basil leaves	cherry tomatoes for garnish

- Put all ingredients except the lettuce greens and the cherry tomatoes into a large mixing bowl and blend well.

- Adjust seasonings to taste.

- Serve on a bed of greens with a few cherry tomatoes to garnish.

Note: For a quick meal, serve with crusty Italian bread and crudites (carrot and celery sticks, sliced red peppers and cucumbers).

Chicken Salad Indienne

*Herbs and spices impart
Eastern flavor*

Planning:
Chill 3 hours or overnight.

Preparation Time:
45 minutes

Yield:
4 to 6 servings

**2 to 3 cups diced cooked
chicken**
**1   13¼-ounce can pineapple
tidbits, drained (1 cup)**
**3   ribs celery, diagonally
sliced**
**4 to 5 scallions, sliced,
including some green
portion**

¼   cup salted peanuts
⅔   cup mayonnaise
**2   tablespoons chopped
chutney**
½   teaspoon grated lime rind
2   tablespoons lime juice
½   teaspoon curry powder
¼   teaspoon salt

- Toss first five ingredients together in a large bowl.
- Combine remaining ingredients in a small bowl, stirring to blend. Pour onto chicken mixture and stir together well. Chill until ready to serve, preferably 3 hours to overnight for flavors to blend.
- Serve on salad greens.

Garden Fresh Chicken Salad

Try cubed pineapple for a change of pace (can be substituted for apples)

Planning:
Salad needs to be refrigerated for several hours prior to serving.

Preparation Time:
5 minutes, 20 minutes

Cooking Time:
1 to 1¼ hours

Yield:
6 servings

2   whole chicken breasts
lemon pepper
dried dill weed (at least
    1 tablespoon to chicken
    breasts plus ½ teaspoon in
    salad)
1   lemon, juiced
salt and pepper, freshly
    ground

1   cup diced celery
1   cup halved seedless grapes
1   cup diced tart apples
mayonnaise
sour cream
1   3-ounce bottle capers
fresh dill, for garnish

- Preheat oven to 325°.

- Lay chicken breasts in baking pan. Sprinkle generously with lemon pepper seasoning and dill weed. Cover pan tightly with foil. Bake for 1 to 1¼ hours.

- Remove chicken from bones and dice. While still warm, sprinkle with lemon juice. Add salt and pepper to taste.

- Add celery, grapes, apples and ½ teaspoon dill weed. Add equal parts mayonnaise and sour cream to chicken mixture — mixing in as you add. Continue until desired consistency is obtained (it should be moist). Fold in capers.

- Chill for several hours. Adjust seasoning and serve.

Tortellini Salad

Robust and tasty

Planning:
Must chill for at least 1 hour

Preparation Time:
30 minutes

Cooking Time:
3 to 5 minutes

Yield:
4 to 6 servings

1   teaspoon salt
1   tablespoon olive oil
1½ pounds fresh cheese or meat-filled tortellini
¼   cup red wine vinegar
1½ teaspoons Dijon-style mustard
salt and pepper to taste
1   cup olive oil
1   tablespoon minced fresh parsley

1   tablespoon fresh snipped dill
2   teaspoons dried basil
6   ounces Black Forest ham, shredded
2   red peppers, cut into julienne strips
½   cup thinly sliced scallions
⅓   cup pine nuts
1½ tablespoons freshly grated Parmesan cheese

- In a large pot, bring to a boil 6 quarts water with 1 teaspoon salt and 1 tablespoon olive oil. Add tortellini. Return to a boil. Cook and stir for 3 to 5 minutes or just until pasta is al dente (cooked but still firm).

- Drain pasta and refresh under cold water. Drain well.

- In a large serving bowl, combine red wine vinegar, mustard, and salt and pepper to taste. Add the olive oil in a stream while whisking until the dressing is well combined.

- Stir in the parsley, dill and basil.

- Add the pasta, ham, red peppers, scallions, pine nuts and Parmesan cheese. Toss gently. Chill covered at least one hour.

Planning:
Make at serving time

Preparation Time:
15 minutes

Yield:
2 servings

Tex-Mex Tuna Salad

Makes a good sandwich, too!

1   6½-ounce can tuna (white tuna packed in water, drained)
½   medium green pepper, diced
2   tablespoons finely chopped red onion
6   ounces Monterey Jack cheese, shredded

⅓   cup oil and vinegar dressing (or to taste)
1   teaspoon dried basil
½   cup sliced black olives
1   cup cherry tomatoes, halved

- Mix all the ingredients in a bowl except the olives and tomatoes. Toss.

- Garnish with black olives and tomatoes.

Note: Serve in pita bread, or on a bed of lettuce with crackers or corn chips.

Seafood Pasta Salad Louis

Serve in a papaya half for a special summer treat.

Planning:
Must be prepared at least 2 hours in advance

Preparation Time:
15 minutes

Yield:
6 to 8 servings

SAUCE LOUIS:
1½ cups mayonnaise
¼ cup chili sauce
¼ cup French dressing
2 tablespoons finely chopped chives
2 tablespoons finely chopped green olives
1 teaspoon prepared horseradish sauce
1 teaspoon Worcestershire sauce
few drops hot pepper sauce

SALAD:
8 ounces cooked pasta swirls
12 ounces cooked salad shrimp
12 ounces lump crab meat
¼ cup diced red onions
¼ cup diced green pepper
½ cup diced celery
salt and pepper to taste
leaf lettuce
black olives for garnish
hard-cooked eggs, quartered, for garnish
red onion rings for garnish
fresh chopped parsley for garnish

- Mix all ingredients for Sauce Louis in a medium bowl.
- Combine pasta, shrimp, crab meat, red onions, green pepper, celery, salt and pepper in a salad bowl. Pour Sauce Louis over all and toss.
- Chill for 1 or 2 hours before serving.

Note: Serve on a bed of leaf lettuce garnished with black olives, hard-cooked eggs, red onion rings and parsley.

grace huntley pugh ©

WILDCLIFF

Vaudeville's Eddie Foy and the Seven Little Foys called New Rochelle home. At the century's turn, Thanhauser Studios produced silent films on Main Street. Today, the city George M. Cohan celebrated in song continues its theatrical tradition in a Victorian gingerbread mansion overlooking Long Island Sound.

Wildcliff, at one time or another in its history a home, museum and a petting zoo, now houses the 101-seat East Coast Arts Theatre. Dedicated to developing new works for the American stage, the theatre premieres plays by the celebrated and the soon-to-be-celebrated.

Harvest Loaf

*The perfect recipe for
home-cooked gifts*

Preparation Time:
15 minutes

Cooking Time:
65 to 75 minutes

Yield:
1 loaf

½   cup shortening
2   eggs
1   cup sugar
¾   cup solid-pack pumpkin
1¾ cups all-purpose flour
1   teaspoon baking soda
1   teaspoon cinnamon

½   teaspoon nutmeg
¼   teaspoon ground cloves
¼   teaspoon ginger
¾   cup semi-sweet chocolate
     chips
¾   cup chopped nuts

- Preheat oven to 350°. Grease a 9x5x3-inch loaf pan.
- Cream shortening and eggs in a large bowl. Gradually add sugar and beat until smooth.
- Blend in pumpkin until smooth.
- Add dry ingredients and mix well.
- Stir in chocolate chips and nuts. Pour mixture into pan.
- Bake for 65 to 75 minutes. Toothpick will come out clean.

Note: While warm, loaf can be topped with confectioners' sugar glaze.

Planning:
Use 4 loaf pans

Preparation Time:
15 minutes

Cooking Time:
1 hour

Yield:
20 slices

Pumpkin Bread

Always a fall favorite!

---

4 cups all-purpose flour	1 teaspoon allspice
3 cups sugar	½ teaspoon ground cloves
2 teaspoons baking soda	1 cup cooking oil
1½ teaspoons salt	1 16-ounce can pumpkin
1 teaspoon baking powder	⅔ cup cold water
1 teaspoon cinnamon	4 eggs
1 teaspoon nutmeg	

- Preheat oven to 350°. Grease and flour 4 small loaf pans.
- Mix flour, sugar, baking soda, salt, baking powder, and spices in large bowl and blend together.
- Pour in cooking oil, the can of pumpkin, and water. Blend well at medium speed using an electric mixer.
- Add the eggs, one at a time, beating well after each addition. Pour batter into pans.
- Bake for 1 hour. Toothpick will come out clean.
- Cool on wire racks.

Autumn Apple Bread

Preparation Time:
15 minutes

Cooking Time:
1 hour

Yield:
1 loaf

A great recipe for extra apples. Just freeze and serve when needed.

2	cups all-purpose flour	½	cup butter, softened
2	teaspoons baking powder	1¼	cups sugar
1	teaspoon salt	2	eggs
1	teaspoon cinnamon	2	cups peeled grated apples
½	teaspoon nutmeg	½	cup crushed pecans

- Preheat oven to 350°. Grease and flour a 9x5x3-inch loaf pan.

- Sift together flour, baking powder, salt, cinnamon and nutmeg.

- In a large bowl, cream butter and sugar together. Beat in eggs one at a time. Stir in sifted ingredients and apples, alternately. Fold in nuts.

- Pour into loaf pan. Bake for one hour.

Preparation Time:
15 minutes

Cooking Time:
1 hour

Yield:
1 loaf

Apple Cheese Bread

Your kitchen never smelled so good.

½   **cup butter, softened**
2   **eggs**
½   **cup sugar**
2   **cups all-purpose flour**
1   **teaspoon baking powder**
½   **teaspoon baking soda**
½   **teaspoon salt**

1½   **cups shredded apples (Granny Smith or Mackintosh)**
¾   **cup shredded Cheddar cheese**
½   **cup chopped walnuts**

- Preheat oven to 350°. Grease a 9x5x3-inch loaf pan.
- In a large bowl, combine butter, eggs, and dry ingredients. Blend until well mixed.
- Stir in shredded apples, Cheddar cheese, and chopped walnuts. Pour mixture into pan.
- Bake for 1 hour. Toothpick will come out clean.
- Cool thoroughly before removing from pan.

Chunky Pineapple Zucchini Bread

Preparation Time:
30 minutes

Cooking Time:
1 hour

Yield:
2 loaves

Moistest-ever zucchini bread

3	eggs	1	teaspoon baking soda
2	cups sugar	1	teaspoon salt
1	cup oil	1	16-ounce can crushed
3	tablespoons vanilla		pineapple, drained
2	cups peeled, grated and well-drained zucchini	1	cup nuts (pecans or walnuts)
3	cups all-purpose flour	½	cup raisins (optional)
1	teaspoon baking powder		

- Preheat oven to 350°. Grease and flour two 9x5x3-inch loaf pans.
- Using a large bowl, beat eggs until fluffy. Add sugar, oil and vanilla and blend well. Add zucchini and blend.
- In a separate bowl, sift together dry ingredients. Add dry ingredients to batter.
- Stir in pineapple, nuts and raisins. Mix well.
- Pour mixture into loaf pans.
- Bake for 1 hour. Toothpick will come out clean.

Planning:
Better if made ahead

Preparation Time:
15 minutes

Cooking Time:
1 hour

Yield:
1 loaf

Banana Bread

*Perfect for weekend guests —
just make during the week.
Your health-conscious friends
will appreciate.*

1½ cups mashed ripe bananas (2 large)	1 teaspoon vanilla extract
¼ cup oil	2 cups whole wheat flour
½ cup honey	¼ cup wheat germ
4 egg whites, lightly beaten	½ teaspoon salt
	1 teaspoon baking powder

- Preheat oven to 350°. Grease well a 9x5x3-inch loaf pan.
- Combine mashed bananas, oil, honey, egg whites and vanilla in a large bowl. Set aside.
- Mix flour, wheat germ, salt, and baking powder in a small bowl.
- Add dry ingredients to banana mixture and beat until smooth. Pour batter in prepared pan.
- Bake for one hour.
- Cool before slicing.

Note: This tastes even better a day or two after it is baked.

Date and Nut Bread

Rich with flavor of the fruit

Preparation Time:
20 minutes

Cooking Time:
45 minutes

Yield:
2 loaves

1   16-ounce package dates, chopped
1½ teaspoons baking soda
1½ cups boiling water
2   tablespoons butter, softened
1¼ cups sugar
2   eggs
1   teaspoon vanilla
3   cups all-purpose flour
1   cup chopped nuts (pecans or walnuts)
pinch of salt

- Preheat oven to 400°.
- In a medium bowl, mix dates and baking soda together. Pour boiling water over dates and soda. Let stand for 10 minutes.
- In a separate large bowl, cream butter and sugar. Add eggs and vanilla and beat until creamy. Add flour, nuts, salt and date mixture. Stir until well mixed.
- Place the mixture in two greased 9x5x3-inch loaf pans, dividing evenly.
- Bake at 400° for 15 minutes. Lower the heat to 350° and bake for 15 minutes. Lower the heat to 300° and bake for 15 minutes or until golden brown.

Preparation Time:
10 minutes

Cooking Time:
50 minutes

Yield:
12 servings

Irish Soda Bread

Don't just serve on St. Patrick's Day

2 **cups sifted all-purpose flour**
1½ **teaspoons baking powder**
¼ **teaspoon baking soda**
½ **cup raisins**
1 **cup buttermilk**

- Preheat oven to 450°. Grease well an 8-inch square pan.
- In a large bowl, blend together flour, baking powder and baking soda. Stir in raisins.
- Add buttermilk, a little bit at a time, to soften dough.
- On a flat, floured board, knead mixture for a few minutes. Place dough in pan.
- Make a slash across the top of dough with a knife, forming a cross.
- Bake at 450° for 10 minutes. Lower heat to 350° and bake for 40 minutes or until golden brown.

Note: Before baking, you can sprinkle a little sugar on the top or brush a little melted butter on the dough.

Spoon Bread

*Serve with a casual dinner.
Great with chili or any
gravy dish.*

Preparation Time:
15 minutes plus 15 minutes
standing

Cooking Time:
1 hour

Yield:
6 servings

1   cup water
2   cups milk
1   teaspoon salt
1   cup corn meal (water ground)

3   eggs, well beaten
¼   cup butter, melted

- Preheat oven to 350°.
- Scald water, milk and salt together in a large saucepan.
- Gradually stir in corn meal and cook over medium heat, stirring constantly until thick.
- Let mixture stand until lukewarm.
- Fold beaten eggs and butter into lukewarm mixture.
- Pour mixture into a well-greased 2-quart casserole.
- Bake for 1 hour. Serve immediately.

Preparation Time:
5 minutes

Cooking Time:
10 minutes

Yield:
40 small biscuits

Herb Biscuits

Dinner rolls with a
difference

4 **tablespoons butter**	1 **teaspoon dill weed**
1 **teaspoon parsley, fresh or dried**	1 **tablespoon sesame seeds**
	1 **teaspoon onion flakes**
1 **tablespoon grated Parmesan cheese**	1 **tube prepared refrigerated biscuits (10 in tube)**

- Preheat oven to 400°.
- Melt butter in a 9-inch round cake or pie pan.
- Sprinkle parsley, Parmesan cheese, dill weed, sesame seeds and onion flakes on pan bottom.
- Cut the 10 biscuits into quarters and gently fit into the pan on top of the herbs and butter.
- Bake for 10 minutes or until golden brown.
- Serve by turning pan upside down onto serving platter.
- Rolls are pulled apart by guests.

Oatmeal Muffins

Preparation Time:
5 minutes

Cooking Time:
25 minutes

Yield:
12 muffins

A nutritious and ever-so-good breakfast selection.

2 cups all-purpose flour	⅔ cup cold cooked oatmeal
3 teaspoons baking powder	1 cup milk
2 tablespoons sugar	2 tablespoons oil
1 egg, well-beaten	

- Preheat oven to 425°. Grease enough muffin tins for 12 muffins or use paper liners.
- In a large bowl, mix together the flour, baking powder and sugar.
- In a separate bowl, combine egg, oatmeal, milk, and oil.
- Add the liquid mixture, a little at a time, to the dry mixture. Stir only enough to moisten the flour completely.
- Pour into muffin tins, filling them ⅔ full.
- Bake for 25 minutes.

Planning:
Freeze for 1 hour

Preparation Time:
10 minutes

Cooking Time:
1 hour

Yield:
3 rolls, 8 slices each

Sour Cream Roll

An easy, but unusual morning or tea pastry

PASTRY:
2   cups all-purpose flour
½   pound butter (2 sticks)

1   cup sour cream

FILLING:*
1   8-ounce package cream
     cheese, softened

¼   cup sugar
1   egg yolk

PASTRY:

- For pastry, cut butter into flour and mix until crumbly. Add sour cream and blend well. Form dough into 3 balls.
- Wrap balls and place in freezer for one hour. When chilled, roll into oblong shape.

FILLING:

- Preheat oven to 350°.
- For cream cheese filling, mix softened cream cheese, sugar and egg yolk. Fill each pastry oblong to the edge of the dough, and roll in jelly roll fashion. Place each roll on a lightly greased baking sheet.
- Bake for one hour.

*For a change, substitute 1 12-ounce can of cake and pastry filling (any variety) apricot, raspberry, prune, almond or poppy seed.

If using canned filling, use a third of filling on each oblong and roll jelly roll fashion. Also, bake for one hour.

The Best Fruit Kuchen

This çake is best served slightly warm. Refresh in oven if desired.

Planning:
May be made in advance

Preparation Time:
15 minutes

Cooking Time:
1 hour

Yield:
10 servings

BATTER:

1	cup sugar	1	teaspoon baking powder
½	cup butter, softened		dash of salt
1	cup flour, sifted	2	eggs

FRUIT TOPPING INGREDIENTS:
Choice of one or more of the following:

Blueberries	Sliced apples
Pitted Cherries	Sliced peaches or nectarines
Halved and pitted Italian plums	

FOR SPRINKLING ON TOP OF FRUIT:

2 to 3 tablespoons sugar, depending on tartness of fruit	1 to 2 teaspoons of lemon juice ½ to 1 teaspoon cinnamon flour (if fruit is juicy)

- Preheat oven to 350°.
- Cream the sugar and butter. Add flour, baking powder, salt and eggs.
- Pour the batter into a 9-inch springform pan.
- Cover the entire surface of the batter in the pan with one or a combination of the fruits suggested above.
- Sprinkle the fruit with the sugar, lemon juice, cinnamon and flour (if fruit is very juicy).
- Bake for 1 hour.

Note: In winter, frozen or canned fruits may be substituted. If using canned fruits, drain and wash off syrup well.

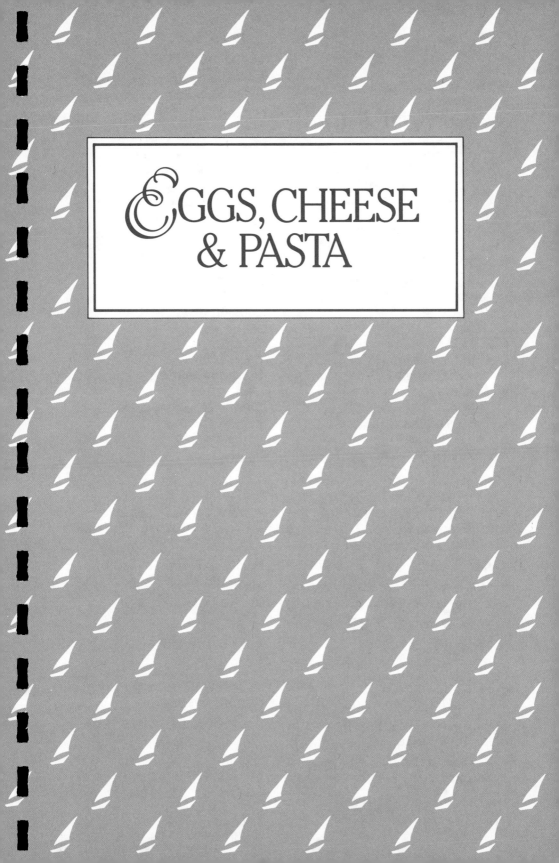

EGGS, CHEESE & PASTA

Golden Brunch Tart

A creamy rich tart with a subtle onion flavor

Planning:
Refrigerate dough 2 hours.
Need a food processor.

Preparation Time:
45 minutes

Cooking Time:
45 minutes

Yield:
8 servings

PASTRY CRUST:

1½ sticks unsalted butter, cut into 12 pieces
1 large egg
2 tablespoons ice water
⅛ teaspoon salt
1¾ cups unbleached flour

FILLING:

2 Spanish onions (½ to ¾ pound), peeled
4 tablespoons unsalted butter
4 slices bacon
6 large eggs
1 cup heavy cream
¼ cup milk
1 teaspoon salt
½ teaspoon nutmeg
ground pepper
1 tomato (4 to 5 ounces), peeled and seeded
2 teaspoons minced fresh basil

PASTRY CRUST:

- Put butter, egg, water and salt into food processor with metal blade. Pulse on/off 7 times then leave on 5 seconds to mix. Small lumps of butter will remain.

- Add flour. Process just until dough begins to form a ball. Stop.

- Shape dough into disk, wrap in plastic and refrigerate at least 2 hours before using. (Can be frozen for later use.)

- Preheat oven to 400°.

- On floured counter, roll out dough to 15-inch diameter.

- Butter bottom of 12-inch quiche pan.

- Put dough into pan, trimming until 1 inch extends out of pan. Fold this inch to form a double thickness on side of pan.

- Line pastry with waxed paper and fill with beans or pellets. Bake for 12 minutes.

- Remove weights and paper. Prick dough with fork and bake 10 minutes more. Remove from oven.

continued

FILLING:
- Turn oven down to 350°.
- Slice onions into medium slices.
- Melt butter in sauté pan over low heat. Add onions. Cover with waxed paper and cook for 10 minutes. Remove waxed paper and cook additional 10 minutes, stirring frequently. Do not let them brown. Set aside.
- Cook bacon until crisp and drain on paper towels.
- In food processor with metal blade, place eggs, cream, milk, salt, nutmeg and pepper to taste. Process on/off 3 times to mix.
- Place onions and bacon in pastry shell.
- Pour egg mixture over filling to ⅛-inch of top of crust. Sprinkle tomato and basil on top.
- Bake for 45 minutes until light brown and puffy. Remove from oven and cool for 10 minutes before serving.

Preparation Time:
10 minutes

Cooking Time:
40 minutes

Yield:
6 servings

Cheese Puff

A luncheon favorite

1 pound Monterey Jack cheese, shredded	1 pint ricotta cheese
1 cup milk	6 eggs, slightly beaten
1 cup flour	½ cup butter, melted

- Preheat oven to 375°.
- Combine Monterey Jack cheese, milk, flour, ricotta cheese, eggs and ¼ cup of butter in a bowl.
- Brush remaining half of melted butter on bottom and sides of 12x7-inch baking dish.
- Pour cheese mixture into dish and bake for 40 minutes or until golden and set.
- Cut into squares and serve.

Sunday Brunch Eggs

Light and elegant

Planning:
Prepare just prior to serving.

Preparation Time:
20 minutes

Cooking Time:
25 minutes

Yield:
6 servings

12 medium asparagus spears
10 eggs
¼ cup heavy cream
salt and freshly ground pepper
2 tablespoons butter
½ cup diced goat cheese (Montrachet)

1 tablespoon minced fresh chives
2 tablespoons butter
2 thin slices prosciutto, cut into 2½"x1½" strips

- Boil asparagus in enough salted water to cover until just tender (about 2 minutes). Drain. Rinse under cold water and drain.
- Whisk eggs, cream, salt and pepper to taste.
- Melt 2 tablespoons butter in 3-quart saucepan over low heat. Add egg mixture and cook, stirring often with a wooden spoon, about 20 minutes, to desired firmness. Add cheese and chives and blend until cheese is melted.
- Melt 2 tablespoons butter in medium skillet over medium heat. Add asparagus and sauté 1 minute. Add prosciutto and stir until heated through.
- Gently stir asparagus mixture into eggs.
- Serve immediately.

Cindy's Overnight Soufflé

Planning:
Refrigerate overnight. Let stand for 30 minutes at room temperature prior to baking. Leftovers can be frozen.

Preparation Time:
25 minutes (day before)

Cooking Time:
45 minutes

Yield:
8 to 10 servings

Perfect for morning company

4	tablespoons unsalted butter	1	pound sharp Cheddar cheese, grated
1	cup sliced fresh mushrooms		salt and pepper to taste
1	large onion, sliced	2	tablespoons snipped fresh dill
16	slices white bread, crusts removed	1	large tomato, peeled and thinly sliced
1	pound lean bacon, cooked and crumbled	6	eggs, lightly beaten
¾	cup diced celery	3	cups light cream
		1	tablespoon Dijon mustard

- Using a large skillet, melt butter over medium heat. Add mushrooms and onions, then brown for 2 minutes or until just tender. Remove with slotted spoon.

- Dip 8 slices of bread in skillet to butter one side. Place bread, butter side down into a 13x9x2-inch baking dish. Place half of the mushrooms, onion, bacon and celery on top of the bread. Then top with half of cheese. Season with salt, pepper and 1 tablespoon of dill.

- Repeat the bread layer and remaining ingredients, but add tomato slices before grated cheese.

- In a small bowl, thoroughly mix eggs, cream and mustard. Pour mixture over casserole. Cover with waxed paper and refrigerate overnight.

- Prior to baking, allow casserole to stand at least 30 minutes at room temperature. Preheat oven to 350°. Bake casserole uncovered for 45 minutes or until souffle-like consistency is reached. Remove from oven and let stand for 5 minutes at room temperature before slicing.

Five Cheese Pie

A cheese-lover's delight

Preparation Time:
30 minutes

Cooking Time:
30 minutes

Yield:
8 servings

¼ **pound Cheddar cheese, grated**
¼ **pound Swiss cheese, grated**
¼ **pound Muenster cheese, grated**
¼ **pound Monterey Jack cheese, grated**
4 **ounces cream cheese, softened**

1 **teaspoon Dijon mustard**
1 **egg, beaten**
2 **8-ounce packages refrigerated crescent rolls**
1 **tablespoon margarine, melted**
sesame seeds

- Preheat oven to 350°.
- Mix grated cheeses with cream cheese in bowl, using hands. Add mustard and beaten egg.
- In a greased 9x13x2-inch pan, press 1 package of rolls to form a crust, pushing dough up on sides of pan. Brush with melted margarine.
- Press cheese mixture into pan. Top with second package of rolls to form top crust.
- Brush with margarine and sprinkle with sesame seeds.
- Bake 30 minutes.

Note: For extra spicy, use Monterey Jack cheese with jalapeño peppers.

Planning:
Need a food processor

Preparation Time:
15 minutes

Cooking Time:
50 minutes

Yield:
4 servings

Cheddar Cheese Soufflé

A rich, golden brown fluffy soufflé

1	tablespoon butter	½	teaspoon salt
¼	cup grated Parmesan cheese	¼	teaspoon white pepper
6	large eggs, room temperature	½	pound sharp Cheddar cheese, cubed
½	cup heavy cream	11	ounces cream cheese, cubed
½	teaspoon mustard		

- Preheat oven to 375°. Use lower-middle rack.
- Butter medium soufflé dish and sprinkle with 2 tablespoons Parmesan cheese.
- Using a food processor fitted with a steel blade, add eggs, cream, mustard, salt and pepper. Process 15 seconds until smooth.
- With motor running, drop Cheddar and cream cheese alternately through feed tube. Process 5 seconds more.
- Pour mixture into soufflé dish and sprinkle with remaining Parmesan cheese. Bake for 50 minutes.
- Serve immediately.

Note: For freshly grated Parmesan cheese, grate in food processor at the beginning of recipe.

Golden Pasta and Rice

A novel combination

Planning:
May sit covered 30 minutes
before serving.

Preparation Time:
10 minutes

Cooking Time:
25 to 30 minutes

Yield:
4 servings

2 tablespoons butter
2 tablespoons margarine
¼ cup minced onion
⅔ cup long grain white rice

⅔ cup spaghetti, broken into
½- to 1-inch pieces
2 cups broth (chicken or beef)

- Melt butter and margarine in a 2-quart saucepan over medium heat. Add onion and sauté 3 minutes.
- Add rice and broken spaghetti and cook, stirring frequently, until golden brown (5 to 7 minutes).
- Add broth, bring to a boil, cover and cook over low heat until liquid is absorbed, about 20 minutes.
- Stir before serving.

Note: White or green spaghetti can be used — or both.

grace huntley pugh ©

LARCHMONT RACE WEEK

It's July, hot and still. The sound looks like a mirror. It must be Larchmont Race Week. Landlubber and seadog unite in prayer for a spanking southwest breeze for Long Island Sound's premier racing event.

During the week the number of boats in the harbor swells from 500 to over 800 as sailors from all along the Connecticut shore, New Jersey, Long Island and Rhode Island participate in the competition and the round of parties ashore.

An annual regatta since 1896, Race Week is hosted by the Larchmont Yacht Club. In 1880, when the club was formed, the majority of its then all male membership lived in New York City and summered in Larchmont. Sailors and spectators arrived on the Larchmont Manor Horse Railway.

In those days, Caldwell H. Colt of Colt Firearms raced the 212', 11" schooner "Dauntless" against railway magnate H.M. Flagler's 108' schooner "Columbia" and the 82' cabin sloop "Titania" owned by C. Oliver Iselin of America's Cup fame.

Today, the boats are smaller and competition is open to young, old, male and female. Larchmont Race Week, a child of Victorian times, has aged gracefully.

Angel Hair Pasta with Smoked Salmon

Preparation Time:
10 minutes

Cooking Time:
45 minutes

Yield:
6 servings

Watch these simple ingredients transform into a distinctive dish.

4   cups tomato sauce (or one 32-ounce jar)
1 to 2 small jars marinated artichoke hearts, drained
1   4-ounce can sliced black olives, drained
1   teaspoon dried hot red pepper flakes or to taste
¼ to ½ pound sliced smoked salmon (lox), sliced
1   pound angel hair pasta
Parmesan cheese, freshly grated

- Combine tomato sauce, artichoke hearts, black olives, red pepper and salmon in a large saucepan. Heat on medium flame for at least 30 to 45 minutes (longer, if possible, to enhance flavor).

- Cook pasta according to package directions. Do not add salt to water. Drain.

- Toss pasta with sauce and salmon.

- Top with Parmesan cheese.

Variation: Replace tomato sauce with ½ to 1 cup olive oil. Cook over medium heat until sizzling hot. Gradually add artichoke hearts, black olives, red pepper and salmon. Heat for 30 to 45 minutes. Add 2 crushed cloves of garlic, if desired. Toss with pasta.

Scallops with Vermicelli

A hearty blend of seafood and pasta

Planning:
Must marinate 45 minutes

Preparation Time:
10 minutes

Cooking Time:
30 minutes

Yield:
4 servings

1½ pounds bay scallops or sea scallops, rinsed and drained
3 tablespoons fresh lemon juice
2 tablespoons minced fresh parsley
1 onion, chopped
1 garlic clove, minced
2 tablespoons olive oil
2 tablespoons unsalted butter
¼ teaspoon crumbled dried oregano
½ teaspoon crumbled dried thyme
2 tablespoons chopped fresh basil
2 14-ounce cans plum tomatoes, drained and chopped (reserve liquid)
¾ pound vermicelli
2 tablespoons heavy cream
freshly grated nutmeg to taste
freshly ground pepper to taste
salt to taste

- In a bowl, combine the scallops (quartered if large), lemon juice and parsley. Marinate at room temperature for 45 minutes.
- In a saucepan, cook the onion and garlic in the oil and 1 tablespoon of the butter until onion is soft.
- Add the oregano, thyme, basil and chopped tomatoes. Simmer covered for 30 minutes, stirring occasionally.
- In boiling salted water, cook vermicelli 7 to 9 minutes until al dente.
- While pasta is cooking, heat remaining tablespoon of butter in a heavy, large skillet until hot. Add scallops and sauté for 2 minutes.
- Add cream, nutmeg, tomato sauce, enough of reserved tomato juice to thin sauce to desired consistency, pepper and salt to taste. Bring to a boil and remove from heat.
- Toss vermicelli and sauce together. Serve immediately.

Linguine with Shrimp and Mussels

Preparation Time:
20 minutes

Cooking Time:
45 minutes

Yield:
4 to 6 servings

*A beautiful main dish that stretches
1 pound of shrimp*

¼ cup chopped onion
2 cloves garlic, pressed
2 to 4 tablespoons olive oil
1 28-ounce can Italian plum tomatoes
1 tablespoon capers
½ teaspoon salt
1 to 2 tablespoons white pepper
1 teaspoon chopped parsley
½ pound black olives, sliced

2 tablespoons olive oil
½ cup white wine
12 large mussels
1 pound medium shrimp, shelled and deveined
¼ teaspoon crushed red pepper
1 pound linguine or angel hair pasta

- Sauté onion and garlic in a bit of olive oil using a large skillet.
- Add to pan tomatoes, capers, salt and pepper and simmer uncovered 20 minutes. Add parsley and olives.
- In a separate saucepan heat 2 tablespoons olive oil.
- Add wine and mussels and steam until mussels open.* Remove and shell.
- In the same saucepan and liquid, steam shrimp until barely done. Shell the shrimp.
- Mix the shrimp and mussels with the sauce in the skillet, along with red pepper.
- Cook linguine and serve together.

*To kill bacteria allow to steam at least 7 minutes.

Preparation Time:
20 minutes

Cooking Time:
20 minutes

Yield:
3 to 4 servings

Angel Hair Pasta and Shrimp

Absolutely heavenly

2	tablespoons butter	¼	cup chopped fresh parsley
2	tablespoons olive oil	½	cup grated Parmesan cheese
¾	pound shrimp, peeled and deveined	½	teaspoon dried basil
2	cloves garlic, crushed	¼	teaspoon red pepper flakes
¾	cup heavy cream	1	8-ounce package angel hair pasta or vermicelli
½	cup white wine		
1	cup tiny peas, thawed		

- In a skillet over medium-high heat, melt butter and oil. Add shrimp and garlic. Cook uncovered about 6 minutes stirring often until shrimp are pink. Remove with slotted spoon to bowl and keep warm.

- Add cream, wine, peas, parsley, ⅓ cup Parmesan cheese, basil and red pepper to skillet. Bring to a boil, reduce heat and simmer 5 to 10 minutes, stirring occasionally until flavors blend.

- Boil pasta 3 to 5 minutes until tender.

- Drain pasta and add to mixture in skillet along with shrimp. Stir until well mixed and heated through.

- Serve with extra Parmesan cheese.

Angel Hair Pasta with Pine Nuts and Sweet Basil

Preparation Time:
30 minutes

Cooking Time:
10 minutes

Yield:
4 servings

This dish is wonderful with broiled salmon or any grilled meat or seafood.

1 head of garlic, pressed
½ to 1 cup olive oil
¼ to ½ cup pine nuts, mashed*
2 tablespoons chopped fresh basil

1 4-ounce can sliced black olives (optional)
1 pound angel hair pasta
¼ cup freshly grated Parmesan cheese

- Combine garlic, olive oil, pine nuts, basil and olives in a large frying pan. Heat over medium heat until hot.
- Cook pasta according to package directions.
- Drain pasta and gradually add oil mixture, tossing. Use more or less to taste.
- Top with Parmesan cheese.

*Wrap pine nuts in plastic and mash with the back of a spoon or other hard object.

Ziti with Chicken and Broccoli in a Cream Sauce

Preparation Time:
10 minutes

Cooking Time:
20 minutes

Yield:
6 servings

Super for a Sunday evening dinner

1 pound chicken breasts, skinned and boned	1 teaspoon dried rosemary
1¼ pounds broccoli, (about one bunch)	⅛ teaspoon red pepper flakes (optional)
½ pound small ziti	1¼ teaspoons dried oregano flakes
2 tablespoons olive oil	1 cup heavy cream
salt and pepper to taste	¼ cup chopped fresh parsley
1 tablespoon minced garlic	½ cup grated Romano or Parmesan cheese
2 cups Italian plum tomatoes, cut into ½-inch pieces	

- Cut chicken breasts into thin strips (about ¼-inch to ½-inch thick). Cut broccoli into small florets (discard thick stems).

- Bring 3 quarts of water to a boil. Add broccoli and cook for 3 minutes. Drain and *reserve* the cooking liquid. Bring liquid to a boil and add ziti. Cook until al dente. Drain ziti and *reserve* ⅓ cup of the liquid.

- Heat olive oil in skillet and add chicken, salt and pepper. Cook over medium heat for 2 minutes. Add garlic. Cook for 1 minute. Add tomatoes, rosemary, red pepper flakes, oregano, and cream. Bring to a boil and simmer for two minutes.

- Add broccoli, ziti, reserved liquid, parsley and cheese. Toss while cooking for one minute. Serve immediately.

Chicken & Pasta with Garden Vegetables

Preparation Time:
1 hour

Cooking Time:
30 minutes

Yield:
4 to 6 servings
(makes 9 cups)

A great after-skiing meal or a warm Sunday evening repast before the work week.

2 tablespoons butter or margarine
1 tablespoon olive oil
1 cup chopped scallions
¾ cup chopped onions
¾ cup 1-inch red pepper strips
¾ cup sliced carrots
½ pound cooked chicken, cut into slivers
¼ cup chopped fresh parsley
2 teaspoons dried basil

2 medium zucchini, diagonally sliced (about 2 cups)
2 large tomatoes, diced
½ cup chicken broth
1 clove garlic, minced
1 teaspoon salt
¼ teaspoon pepper
8 ounces rotelli pasta
2 tablespoons butter or margarine, melted
⅓ cup grated Romano cheese

- Heat 2 tablespoons butter and olive oil in skillet. Add scallions, onions, red pepper, carrots, chicken, parsley and basil. Cover and simmer ten minutes.

- Add zucchini, tomatoes, broth, garlic, salt and pepper. Cover and cook 15 to 20 minutes or until all vegetables are tender.

- While vegetables are cooking, cook pasta as directed on package and drain.

- Pour melted butter over pasta, sprinkle with cheese and toss.

- Pour warm vegetable mixture over pasta. Toss and serve.

Preparation Time:
10 minutes

Cooking Time:
10 minutes

Yield:
4 servings

Fettuccine with Spinach and Sun-Dried Tomatoes

The Italian colors at their best!

2	garlic cloves
1	10-ounce bag spinach, washed and dried
4	ounces drained, oil-packed sun-dried tomatoes (approximately ½ cup)
12	ounces fresh fettuccine noodles

$\frac{1}{3}$ cup pine nuts (pignoli)
$\frac{1}{3}$ cup olive oil
$\frac{1}{2}$ cup coarsely grated Parmesan cheese
salt and pepper to taste

- Thinly slice garlic.
- Coarsely chop spinach leaves.
- Cut sun-dried tomatoes into bite-sized pieces.
- Prepare fettuccine as directed on label.
- In a 12-inch skillet, toast pine nuts, stirring until browned. Remove and set aside.
- In same skillet, heat oil and brown garlic. Remove garlic from oil.
- Add spinach and sun-dried tomatoes to oil over medium heat, and cook just until spinach wilts.
- Drain fettuccine, place in warmed bowl and toss with spinach mixture, pine nuts and Parmesan cheese.
- Add salt and pepper to taste.
- Serve immediately.

Pasta Primavera

Preparation Time:
25 minutes

Cooking Time:
15 minutes

Yield:
4 servings

*Everything you want in
a primavera*

2 stalks celery, chopped	2 carrots, grated
1 yellow onion, chopped	20 pea pods
1 medium green pepper, chopped	4 plum tomatoes, diced
¼ cup olive oil	Italian seasoning, to taste
2 garlic cloves, minced	½ cup white wine
4 ounces fresh mushrooms, sliced	salt and pepper, to taste
1 medium zucchini, sliced thin	red pepper flakes, to taste
	1 pound angel hair pasta
	4 ounces mozzarella cheese, grated

- Sauté celery, onion and green pepper in olive oil. Add garlic.
- Add mushrooms, zucchini, carrots, pea pods and tomatoes. Cook until softened.
- Add Italian seasoning, white wine, salt and pepper and red pepper flakes to taste.
- Cook the pasta according to directions and drain.
- Mix pasta with vegetables and mozzarella cheese and serve.

Planning:
Marinate at least 2 hours or overnight

Preparation Time:
10 minutes

Cooking Time:
10 minutes

Yield:
4 to 6 servings

Pasta with Vodka Sauce

Easy gourmet

½	cup vodka	1	cup light cream
1	teaspoon to 1 tablespoon crushed red pepper flakes or to taste	½	cup butter
		1	cup tomato sauce
		1	pound pasta, cooked

- Mix vodka and crushed red pepper. Let it sit overnight or at least 2 hours.
- In a non-stick pan, heat vodka mixture. Light mixture and let it burn until flame goes out.
- Add cream and butter and heat thoroughly.
- Add tomato sauce, and again heat thoroughly.
- Add pasta, mix and serve.

Cold Noodles in Sesame Sauce

Perfect accompaniment to any grilled chicken.

Planning:
Chill pasta 2 hours.

Preparation Time:
15 minutes

Cooking Time:
10 minutes

Yield:
8 servings

1 pound vermicelli
2 tablespoons oriental sesame oil
1 1-inch piece of fresh ginger (cut in pieces)
4 garlic cloves
½ cup peanut butter
½ cup water
4 tablespoons soy sauce

4 tablespoons tahini (sesame seed paste)
2 tablespoons peanut oil
2 tablespoons sherry
4 teaspoons white vinegar
1 tablespoon sugar
½ teaspoon Chinese chili oil or red pepper flakes
3 to 4 scallions, chopped

- Cook pasta according to package directions. Drain well and add sesame oil, tossing lightly to coat. Cover and chill at least 2 hours.

- Place all sauce ingredients — ginger, garlic, peanut butter, water, soy sauce, tahini, peanut oil, sherry, vinegar, sugar, Chinese chili oil or red pepper flakes in food processor. Mix with steel blade until sauce mixture is smooth.

- Add sauce to chilled pasta, tossing well to coat.

- Garnish with chopped scallions.

Note: Nice with Chicken Yakitori (see page 186).

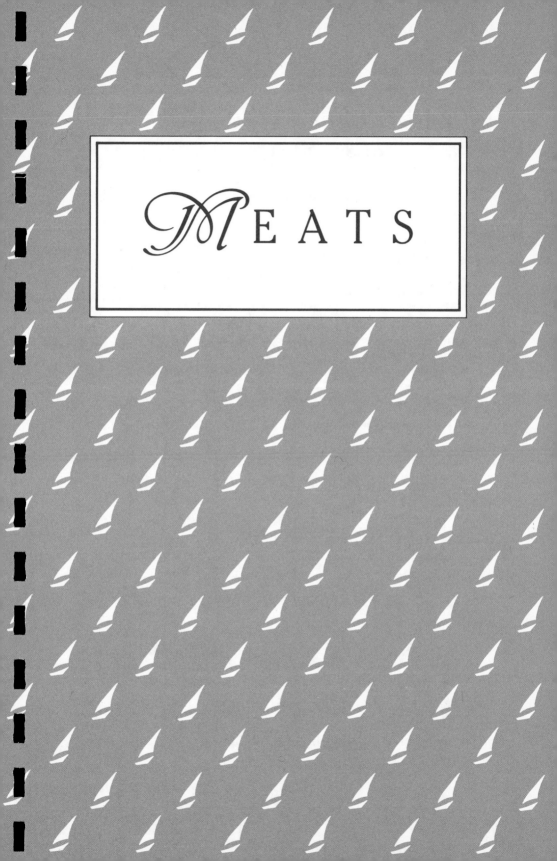

MEATS

Grilled Beef Fillet with Blue Cheese Sauce

Preparation Time:
20 minutes

Cooking Time:
20 to 25 minutes

Yield:
6 to 8 servings

Decadently delicious!

5½ pounds beef fillet, trimmed
salt and pepper to taste

2 tablespoons unsalted butter

BLUE CHEESE SAUCE:
¾ cup Madeira
2 tablespoons minced shallots
1 cup heavy cream
½ cup beef broth
½ cup unsalted butter, softened

6 ounces blue cheese, softened
cayenne pepper to taste
salt and pepper to taste
1 cup sour cream
paprika

- Start grill.
- Tie beef fillet crosswise at 1-inch intervals with kitchen string and pat dry.
- Sprinkle beef with salt and pepper and rub with 2 tablespoons unsalted butter.
- Grill beef over bed of glowing coals about 3 inches from heat for 20 to 25 minutes (for rare meat), turning frequently.
- Transfer beef to cutting board, let it stand 15 minutes, and remove and discard string.
- Cut the beef into ½-inch slices and serve with blue cheese sauce.

BLUE CHEESE SAUCE:

- In a stainless steel or enamel saucepan, combine Madeira with minced shallots and reduce the mixture over medium-high heat to about 2 tablespoons.
- Add heavy cream and beef broth and reduce the liquid over medium heat to about 1 cup.
- In a bowl, cream together butter and blue cheese until mixture is smooth.

continued

- Whisk the cheese mixture, a little at a time, into the sauce in the saucepan and simmer for 3 minutes.
- Add cayenne pepper and salt and pepper to taste.
- Cool mixture to room temperature. Add 1 cup sour cream.
- Transfer sauce to a pitcher and sprinkle with paprika.

Planning:
Must prepare 1 to 2 hours ahead

Preparation Time:
15 minutes

Cooking Time:
20 minutes

Yield:
4 servings

Steak au Poivre

Filet at its finest

3 tablespoons whole black peppercorns	2 tablespoons unsalted butter
4 filet mignon steaks (6 to 8 ounces each)	4 to 6 tablespoons cognac
6 tablespoons olive oil, divided use	1 cup beef bouillon
salt	1½ tablespoons minced shallots
	1 cup whipping cream

- Crush peppercorns coarsely.
- Remove fat from steaks. Dry meat with paper towels. Rub meat with oil (about 4 tablespoons) on top, bottom and sides. Cover meat with peppercorns and press into meat. Allow steaks to sit 1 to 2 hours before cooking.
- Preheat oven to 200°.
- Salt steaks lightly. Over medium-high heat, melt butter and 2 tablespoons oil in frying pan. Add meat and cook both sides until desired doneness (approximately 10 minutes).
- Add cognac; when hot, ignite with a match. Spoon flaming sauce over steaks until fire goes out.
- Remove meat and put in oven to warm.
- Add bouillon and shallots to frying pan over high heat. Scrape pan frequently. Reduce liquid to ⅔. Add cream and reduce further. Add steak juices and cook an additional 2 minutes.
- Serve sauce over steaks or on the side.

Ginger Beef Kabobs

Marinade enhances beef

Planning:
Marinate one hour or overnight

Preparation Time:
10 minutes

Cooking Time:
12 to 15 minutes

Yield:
4 servings

½ cup vegetable oil
½ cup Burgundy wine
2 tablespoons finely snipped candied ginger OR 1 tablespoon ground ginger
2 tablespoons ketchup
2 tablespoons molasses
½ teaspoon salt
½ teaspoon curry powder
½ teaspoon pepper
1 large clove garlic, minced
1 pound sirloin steak, cut in 1-inch cubes
1 green pepper, cut in pieces

- In a glass bowl or shallow dish, combine all ingredients except meat and green pepper.
- Add beef and let stand at room temperature for 1 hour or refrigerate overnight.
- Start grill or preheat broiler.
- Remove beef cubes and arrange on skewers with green pepper pieces.
- Cook over medium-hot coals for 12 to 15 minutes, brushing several times with marinade.

Note: Can also be used as a marinade for flank steak or London broil.

grace huntley pugh ©

CARTOON MUSEUM

His neighbors in what is now Rye Brook nicknamed it "Ward's Folly." But William Evans Ward persevered and in 1876 completed construction on the world's first home built entirely of reinforced concrete. The millionaire manufacturer of screws, nuts and bolts tested his theory of using light iron beams and rods to reinforce the poured-in-place concrete by resting a 26 ton weight on the second floor for six months. Ward Castle stood firm with not so much as a groan.

The family continued in the castle for two more generations, producing a king of sorts, William Lukens Ward, Republican Committee Chairman of Westchester, whose patronage was sought for all political appointments, expenditures and court rulings in the county.

Placed on the National Register of Historic Places in 1976, Ward Castle was purchased the following year by the Museum of Cartoon Art. The collection containing over 60,000 pieces of original cartoon art, 10,000 books and hundreds of hours of film and video tape draws over 15,000 visitors to the museum annually. Yet, "Ward's Folly" stands firm.

Grilled Flank Steak Tournedos

Preparation Time:
15 minutes

Cooking Time:
15 minutes

Yield:
4 servings

Bacon adds extra flavor

1 large flank steak	1 teaspoon garlic salt
instant non-seasoned meat tenderizer	½ teaspoon ground pepper
½ pound bacon (cooked, but not crisp)	2 tablespoons chopped parsley

- Preheat grill.
- Score meat diagonally and sprinkle on both sides with tenderizer.
- Sprinkle one side with garlic salt, pepper and parsley and top with bacon slices placed lengthwise.
- Starting at the narrow end, roll meat jelly-roll fashion and secure with toothpicks at one-inch intervals.
- Slice through steak roll to make pinwheel slices about 1-inch thick.
- Grill slices about 7 to 8 minutes on each side (about 15 minutes total).

Grilled Beef Slices

Preparation Time:
10 minutes

Cooking Time:
15 minutes

Yield:
6 servings

Moistest-ever London broil

6 scallions, finely chopped	2 tablespoons dry sherry
5 garlic cloves, crushed	2 tablespoons white sesame seeds
½ cup soy sauce	pepper to taste
2 tablespoons vegetable oil	2 pounds London broil
2 tablespoons brown sugar	

- Preheat grill.
- Combine all marinade ingredients in a shallow pan and mix well. Add beef and turn to coat.
- Grill 5 to 7 minutes per side over medium flame.
- Slice beef thinly and serve heated marinade as a sauce.

Preparation Time:
20 minutes

Cooking Time:
30 minutes

Yield:
8 to 10 servings

Beef Stroganov

Always elegant

1	6 to 7 pound beef fillet	2	medium-sized onions, grated (retain juice)
½	cup all-purpose flour		
½	cup butter	1	cup heavy cream
2	tablespoons whiskey	1	sprig fresh dill, chopped
½	cup red wine		

- Cut the beef into strips, ¼-inch thick and 2 inches long.
- Sprinkle beef with flour. In a large skillet brown beef in hot butter. Pour whiskey over meat and ignite. Remove from heat until flame extinguishes.
- Return to medium heat and add red wine, grated onion, and onion juice. Heat for 15 minutes without bringing to a boil.
- Fold some of the warm sauce into the heavy cream so that cream does not curdle.
- Blend heavy cream mixture with sauce and heat for 3 minutes over medium heat.
- Garnish with dill.

Note: Serve with white rice.

Daube Flambé au Cognac

Flame adds flavor

Preparation Time:
1 hour

Cooking Time:
2½ hours

Yield:
8 to 10 servings

4	pounds shoulder or chuck steak, cut into 1-inch cubes	3	garlic cloves, chopped
4	tablespoons vegetable oil	¼	teaspoon parsley
2	large onions, sliced	¼	teaspoon thyme
4	ounces cognac	¼	teaspoon laurel
2 to 3	tablespoons flour	¼	teaspoon savory
3	pints dry white wine		salt and pepper to taste
6	medium-sized tomatoes, chopped	1	8-ounce can black olives, pitted and drained

- Preheat oven to 350°.

- Brown the beef in vegetable oil with the 2 large sliced onions over medium heat in batches.

- Drain juices from meat and onion.

- Pour the cognac over the meat and ignite while stirring. Remove from heat until flame extinguishes.

- Sprinkle with flour and pour in the white wine. Add the tomatoes, garlic, herbs and salt and pepper to taste. Bring to a boil and let cook over medium flame for 20 to 30 minutes.

- Cover and simmer in oven for at least 2 hours. Check occasionally for sticking and to make sure that mixture is not boiling but only bubbling very slightly.

- Add the olives fifteen minutes before serving.

Note: Tomato concentrate may be added if sauce needs to be thickened.

When preparing this dish in advance, make sure to let it simmer for about 30 minutes prior to serving.

Planning:
Can be made ahead

Preparation Time:
30 minutes

Cooking Time:
2 hours

Yield:
6 to 8 servings

Beef Stew with Red Wine

A perfect autumn selection.
Make ahead for weekend guests.

3½ pounds beef sirloin
12 small white onions (can use frozen)
12 small carrots (can use frozen)
⅛ pound salt pork or other shortening
2 tablespoons flour
1 6-ounce can tomato paste

1 cup beef bouillon broth
1 cup red wine
1 teaspoon salt
1 bay leaf
¾ teaspoon pepper
6 to 8 whole peppercorns
¼ teaspoon basil
fresh parsley for garnish

- Preheat oven to 250°.
- Cut sirloin into cubes.
- Brown meat, onions, carrots in the fat in a skillet. Transfer to a 3-quart casserole with a slotted spoon.
- Drain surplus fat from skillet.
- Sprinkle flour in the skillet. Add tomato paste, bouillon and wine, gradually stirring until thickened. If more liquid is necessary, add wine and bouillon alternately.
- Add salt, bay leaf, pepper, peppercorns and basil. Simmer a few minutes then pour over contents of casserole.
- Place in oven for 2 hours, covered.

Daube de Bouef

---

*A hearty offering for a cold
winter night*

Planning:
Marinate 2½ hours

Preparation Time:
45 minutes

Cooking Time:
1 hour

Yield:
8 to 10 servings

3 pounds lean stewing beef, cubed
1 cup dry white or red wine
¼ cup brandy
½ cup olive or vegetable oil
2 large onions, peeled and thinly sliced
4 carrots, peeled and diced
2 bay leaves
1 teaspoon dried thyme
¼ cup chopped fresh parsley
salt and freshly ground pepper to taste

½ cup diced thick bacon
2 garlic cloves, crushed
3 medium-sized tomatoes, peeled, seeded and chopped
1 cup sliced fresh mushrooms
1 small strip orange peel
½ teaspoon dried rosemary
12 pitted black olives

- Put the beef, wine, brandy, ¼ cup olive oil, 1 sliced onion, 2 diced carrots, bay leaves, thyme and 2 tablespoons parsley in a large bowl. Season with salt and pepper. Marinate about 2½ hours, stirring occasionally.

- When ready to cook, put the bacon, garlic, remaining 2 tablespoons of oil, 1 sliced onion and 2 diced carrots in a large Dutch oven and sauté for 5 minutes.

- Take the meat from the marinade and wipe dry. Reserve the marinade. Brown a few pieces at a time in the oil drippings, pushing the vegetables aside.

- When all the meat is browned, mix in the tomatoes, mushrooms, orange peel and rosemary. Season with salt and pepper.

- Pour in the reserved marinade, including the vegetables. Cover and cook slowly for 1 hour.

- Stir in the olives after cooking for 30 minutes.

- When the cooking is completed, add the remaining parsley. Remove and discard the bay leaves.

Preparation Time:
10 minutes

Cooking Time:
10 minutes

Yield:
2 to 3 servings

Chinese Beef with Snow Peas

All you need is rice to make this dish a meal.

1	pound beef steak or flank steak	1	teaspoon sugar
4	tablespoons soy sauce	¼	pound pea pods
1	tablespoon cornstarch	4	tablespoons cooking oil
1	tablespoon dry sherry	½	teaspoon salt
		1	slice ginger root

- Cut beef into thin ¼-inch slices about 2-inches long.
- Mix beef with soy sauce, cornstarch, sherry and sugar and set aside.
- Rinse pea pods and dry on cloth.
- Put two tablespoons oil in hot skillet over high flame. Add salt first and then the pea pods. Stir constantly until pods turn darker green (less than one minute). Remove pods and spread on a plate.
- In the same skillet, add remaining oil and ginger root. Stir in beef mixture and turn constantly until beef is almost cooked (not over two minutes).
- Add pea pods, mix and serve immediately.

Shredded Beef Tortillas with Mexican Red Sauce

Preparation Time:
1½ hours

Cooking Time:
55 minutes, meat
15 to 20 minutes, sauce
10 to 15 minutes, tortillas

Yield:
4 servings

Lighter than the usual Mexican fare

MEAT:
2 pounds beef, cut into 1-inch cubes	2 cloves garlic, chopped
4 cups water	2 teaspoons salt
½ medium onion, chopped	4 tablespoons oil
	2 tablespoons minced onion

SAUCE:
5 tablespoons oil	2* 4½-ounce cans Mexican green chilies (mild), cut into 1-inch strips
1 small onion, sliced thin	
1 28-ounce can tomatoes, chopped (retain liquid)	

10 to 12 corn tortillas
8 ounces Monterey Jack cheese, shredded

MEAT:

- Place cubed beef into 2-quart saucepan with water, chopped onion, garlic and salt. Bring to a boil, cover and simmer for 55 minutes.
- Drain liquid and shred beef in food processor or pull apart using two forks.
- Heat oil. Add meat and minced onion. Cook until meat is crisp, about 10 minutes.

SAUCE:

- Heat oil in 4-quart saucepan.
- Add onions and sauté until soft (5 to 10 minutes).
- Add tomatoes (with liquid) and chilies and cook over high flame with lid (slightly askew) to prevent splattering.
- Cook, stirring frequently, 15 to 20 minutes until almost all liquid has evaporated.

continued

ASSEMBLY:
- Preheat oven to 400°.
- Heat corn tortillas (or fry).
- Place 1 tablespoon sauce on open tortilla and 2 tablespoons of meat. Close tortilla and top with 2 tablespoons cheese. Place on a lightly greased cookie sheet.
- Heat in oven for 10 to 15 minutes or until cheese melts.

* For hot sauce, substitute 1 can mild chilies with 4 to 6 jalapeño chilies cut into 1-inch strips, seeds discarded.

Note: Excellent with Mexican rice and refried beans.

Preparation Time:
25 minutes

Cooking Time:
3 hours

Yield:
4 servings

Arizona Chili

Zesty!

½ tablespoon olive oil
1 pound ground sirloin
1 28-ounce can Italian plum tomatoes, puréed
1 cup water
2 tablespoons onion, minced
2 tablespoons chili powder
2 tablespoons celery flakes
1 teaspoon oregano
½ teaspoon garlic powder
¾ teaspoon ground cumin
¼ teaspoon curry powder
½ teaspoon dry mustard
⅛ teaspoon red pepper
1 4-ounce can mild green chilies, chopped
½ to 1 teaspoon canned jalapeño chilies (hot), chopped
salt to taste
sour cream for garnish

- Heat oil until hot in a 2-quart ceramic saucepan. Add beef and brown, about 10 minutes.
- Add puréed tomatoes, water, onion, chili powder, celery flakes, oregano, garlic powder, cumin, curry powder, mustard, red pepper and chilies. Heat to boiling.
- Reduce heat, cover and simmer. Cook for 2½ to 3 hours, stirring often. Salt to taste.

Note: Red kidney beans may be added the last 15 minutes of cooking, if desired.

Flame Thrower Chili

Even better the next day

Planning:
Can be made ahead

Preparation Time:
30 minutes

Cooking Time:
2 hours

Yield:
6 to 8 servings

3	pounds top round beef, cut into ½-inch cubes	1	teaspoon ground cumin
6	tablespoons corn oil	1	teaspoon red pepper flakes
2	cups coarsely chopped onion	1	6-ounce can tomato paste
2	tablespoons finely chopped garlic	4	cups beef stock
3	tablespoons chili powder (or to taste)	½	teaspoon salt
1	teaspoon oregano	½	teaspoon pepper
		1½	cups canned kidney beans, drained (optional)

- Dry meat. Put 4 tablespoons oil in skillet and heat until hot. Add meat and brown. Remove from skillet and transfer to a large heat-proof casserole.
- Add remaining oil to skillet and sauté onions and garlic 4 to 5 minutes. Remove from heat.
- Add chili powder, oregano, cumin and pepper flakes and stir well.
- Add tomato paste and beef stock and mix well.
- Add to meat in casserole and add salt and pepper. Bring to a boil, stirring constantly. Partially cover pot.
- Turn heat low and simmer until beef is tender (about one hour and 45 minutes).
- Add beans 15 minutes before meat is done.

grace huntley pugh

WALTER'S

If the truth were known, Mamaroneck youth away from home for the first time, miss Walter's dogs more than Mom's cooking. Postcards, some over twenty years old, taped to the windows of the famous hot dog stand carry postmarks from college towns across the country, summer sojourns abroad, and even Saigon. Their messages bear testimony to the world's most fabulous frank.

On Palmer Avenue since 1928, the stand has been a family business for over seventy years. It was started by Walter Warrington in 1919 on the Boston Post Road near the Richbell Road intersection. The stand's unique architecture (of all things, Chinese Carp) merited a Westchester County Historic Architecture Award.

Brisket with Prunes & Apricots

Preparation Time:
15 minutes

Cooking Time:
4 hours

Yield:
4 to 6 servings

A festive approach to a budget cut of meat

2   onions, sliced
1   2 to 3 pound lean beef brisket
1   12-ounce can of beer (or more)
1   cup dried pitted prunes
1   cup dried apricots
3   tablespoons brown sugar
2   tablespoons orange marmalade (preferably bitter)

1   tablespoon brandy
1   tablespoon grated lemon peel
juice of one lemon
¾   teaspoon grated ginger
½   teaspoon cinnamon
½   teaspoon Worcestershire sauce
½   teaspoon freshly ground pepper

- Preheat oven to 350°.
- Cut a piece of aluminum foil large enough to wrap brisket. Sprinkle half of the onion over the foil in a layer about the same size as brisket.
- Set brisket on top of onion. Sprinkle remaining onion over top. Seal tightly. Set in large shallow pan. Roast three hours.
- Combine 12 ounces of beer with remaining ingredients in large saucepan and bring to boil over medium-high heat. Remove from heat.
- Discard foil and spread fruit mixture atop brisket.*
- Reduce oven temperature to 300°. Cover pan and continue roasting one hour, adding more beer to pan if sauce appears dry.
- Transfer brisket to heated platter and surround with fruit and sauce.

*Can be made ahead to this point. It is best when made ahead a day or two. Avoid overcooking when reheating so the fruit does not get mushy.

Butterflied Leg of Lamb

Planning:
Marinate 1 hour

Preparation Time:
5 minutes

Cooking Time:
35 minutes

Yield:
6 to 8 servings

Perfect choice if rain threatens your barbecue.
Equally delicious grilled or roasted.

2	tablespoons Dijon mustard	2	tablespoons olive oil
½	teaspoon salt	1	clove garlic, crushed
¼	teaspoon pepper	⅓	cup lemon juice
4	tablespoons brown sugar	1	leg of lamb, butterflied
2	tablespoons soy sauce		

- In a small bowl, combine mustard, salt, pepper, brown sugar, soy sauce, olive oil, garlic and lemon juice.
- Spread over meat and marinate for one hour.
- Preheat oven to 450° or light barbecue.
- Roast for 35 minutes or until done or grill on barbecue 15 to 20 minutes per side.

Barbecued Butterflied Lamb

Planning:
Marinate 4 to 12 hours

Preparation Time:
5 minutes

Cooking Time:
45 minutes

Yield:
10 servings

An easy cookout choice

8	ounces Dijon mustard	garlic
8	ounces peanut oil	1 leg of lamb, butterflied
8	ounces soy sauce	

- Prepare marinade by mixing mustard, oil and soy sauce together. Crush garlic and mix into marinade.
- Put meat into large enough dish to hold meat and marinade. Pour marinade over lamb and marinate 4 to 12 hours, turning occasionally.
- Barbecue for 45 minutes for medium-rare lamb.
- Slice on the diagonal, as for London broil.

Grilled Lamb with Herbs

Always a summer favorite

Planning:
Marinate overnight

Preparation Time:
15 minutes

Cooking Time:
20 to 40 minutes

Yield:
8 servings

1   cup dry red wine
½   cup olive oil
2   tablespoons snipped parsley
2   tablespoons chopped chives
½   teaspoon Worcestershire sauce
¼   teaspoon ground black pepper
¼   teaspoon marjoram
¼   teaspoon rosemary
¼   teaspoon thyme
2   cloves garlic, chopped fine
1   leg of lamb, boned and butterflied

- Combine all ingredients except lamb to make marinade. Pour over lamb and marinate overnight in refrigerator.
- Light grill or preheat oven to 450°.
- Barbecue 10 to 20 minutes per side, depending on preference for doneness, basting frequently. Or roast in oven for 30 to 40 minutes.
- Carve diagonally on grain.

Preparation Time:
25 minutes

Cooking Time:
18 to 20 minutes per pound

Yield:
6 to 8 servings

Roast Leg of Lamb

A well-seasoned old favorite

1   leg of lamb, 6 to 7 pounds
butter
1   lemon, juiced
6   minced shallots
1   garlic clove, minced
1½ cups fresh bread crumbs
1   teaspoon fresh or dried
    thyme

1   teaspoon fresh or dried
    parsley
1   teaspoon fresh or dried
    basil
1 or 2 bay leaves
buttered brown paper
additional lemon juice

- Preheat oven to 300°.
- Rub lamb with butter and lemon juice. Sprinkle on shallots and garlic.
- Blend bread crumbs and herbs. Rub lamb with mixture, reserving about ½ cup.
- Put in a pan and cover with buttered brown paper.
- Roast 18 to 20 minutes per pound.
- Remove paper. Top with herb mixture and lemon juice. Brown under broiler and serve.

Imperial Lamb

---

*The herb coating makes
the difference.*

Planning:
Needs ½ hour resting period
after roasting

Preparation Time:
10 minutes

Cooking Time:
20 minutes, then 30 minutes
per pound

Yield:
6 to 8 servings

1   **6 to 7 pound leg of lamb —
boned, rolled and tied**

MARINADE:

¼	**cup oil**	¼	**teaspoon thyme**
⅓	**cup lemon juice**		**salt & pepper to taste**
2	**cloves garlic, pressed**		

GARLIC HERB COATING:

2	**teaspoons melted butter**	¼	**teaspoon thyme**
⅓	**cup bread crumbs**	1	**tablespoon chopped**
1	**clove garlic, pressed**		**parsley**

- Preheat oven to 425°.
- Combine marinade ingredients and blend well.
- Place lamb in roasting pan and baste with marinade several minutes, pouring it all on lamb.
- Roast at 425° for 20 minutes, then lower temperature to 300°. Continue roasting until meat thermometer registers approximately 170° for medium.
- Baste frequently during baking time.
- In a bowl, combine Garlic Herb Coating and stir until blended.
- About 30 minutes before lamb is done, carefully sprinkle Garlic Herb Coating over lamb.
- Continue baking until thermometer registers doneness.
- For gravy, remove lamb from pan and strain juices. Remove all fat.
- The lamb will be easier to slice if it has a ½ hour resting period out of the oven. Serve with gravy.

Preparation Time:
15 minutes

Cooking Time:
25 minutes

Yield:
4 to 6 servings

Veal Scallops with Prosciutto and Sage

Authentic Italian in little time

1	pound thin sliced veal cutlets	1	cup chicken broth
5	tablespoons flour	¼	cup cooking sherry
½	teaspoon rubbed sage	¼	pound sliced prosciutto ham, cut into ½-inch strips
	butter or margarine	¼	teaspoon pepper
	olive or salad oil	2	teaspoons minced parsley

- With meat mallet, pound each cutlet to about ¼-inch thickness. Cutlets should be about five-inch by four-inch pieces.
- On waxed paper, mix flour and sage and evenly coat cutlets.
- In a 12-inch skillet over medium-high heat, cook two tablespoons butter and two tablespoons oil until hot. Add veal cutlets, a few pieces at a time. Cook until browned on both sides, about two minutes, removing cutlets as they brown. Add more butter or oil if necessary.
- To drippings remaining in skillet, add broth and sherry. Over high heat, heat to boiling, stirring to loosen brown bits from skillet.
- Return cutlets to skillet and add prosciutto and heat through.
- Arrange meat and sauce on warm platter. Sprinkle with pepper and parsley.

Veal Vesuvio

An elegant and attractive company dish yet simple in execution.

Preparation Time:
10 minutes

Cooking Time:
30 minutes

Yield:
4 servings

6 slices veal scallopine, sliced from the leg	6 lean slices prosciutto
flour	6 thin slices mozzarella cheese
1 egg, beaten	2 tablespoons tomato sauce
3 tablespoons butter	sage
1 small eggplant, sliced thin (enough to cover veal slices)	¼ cup dry white wine
	¼ cup sherry
	¼ cup chicken stock

- Pound veal, dredge in flour and dip in beaten egg. Sauté veal in butter in a large frying pan until lightly browned. Remove from skillet.

- Add eggplant to the skillet and sauté. Remove from skillet. Drain carefully between heavy paper towels.

- Place veal back into skillet and top each piece with eggplant, prosciutto, mozzarella cheese, 1 teaspoon tomato sauce and a sprinkle of sage.

- Mix white wine, sherry and chicken stock and place in skillet. Simmer, covered, 8 to 10 minutes.

- Serve immediately.

Italian Veal Roll-Ups

Preparation Time:
30 minutes

Cooking Time:
30 minutes

Yield:
3 to 4 servings

A delightful combination

2 pounds veal cutlets (8 slices)
flour
1 garlic clove, minced
3 tablespoons minced parsley
pinch of salt and pepper
3 slices lean ham, finely diced

6 tablespoons grated Parmesan cheese
6 tablespoons sweet butter, melted
2 tablespoons olive oil
½ cup chopped Italian plum tomatoes

- Pound veal until thin. Sprinkle with flour and shake off excess. Lay veal on flat surface.
- Mix garlic, parsley, salt, pepper, ham, 3 tablespoons of the cheese and 2 tablespoons melted butter in a bowl.
- Brush veal with 1 to 2 tablespoons butter, and spread 1 heaping teaspoon of the mixture down center of veal. Roll each piece and secure with a toothpick.
- Heat oil and remaining butter. Add veal rolls and brown nicely on all sides.
- Add tomatoes, cover and cook slowly 25 to 30 minutes.
- Sprinkle with remaining cheese and serve.

Veal Forestier

Preparation Time:
10 minutes

Cooking Time:
50 minutes

Yield:
4 servings

This dish has a lovely delicate flavor and is simple to prepare.

1	pound veal cutlets, about $\frac{1}{4}$-inch thick	2	tablespoons water
$\frac{1}{4}$	cup flour	$\frac{3}{4}$	teaspoon salt
4	tablespoons butter or margarine		dash pepper
$\frac{1}{2}$	pound mushrooms, sliced	1	tablespoon chopped parsley
$\frac{1}{2}$	cup dry vermouth		sautéed cherry tomatoes
			parsley sprigs

- Pound veal to $\frac{1}{8}$-inch thickness and cut into 3-inch by 2-inch pieces. On waxed paper coat cutlets lightly with flour.
- In a 10-inch skillet over medium-high heat melt butter. Cook the veal a few pieces at a time until lightly browned on both sides. Remove pieces as they brown and add more butter if necessary.
- Add mushrooms, vermouth, water, salt and pepper to the skillet. Heat to boiling and reduce heat to low. Cover and simmer five minutes or until mushrooms are tender.
- Return the veal to the skillet and heat through. Stir in the chopped parsley.
- Arrange the veal on a platter with tomatoes. Garnish with parsley sprigs.

Preparation Time:
15 minutes

Cooking Time:
40 minutes

Yield:
4 servings

Veal Scallopine a la Madeira

A foolproof company dish

¼   **pound mushrooms, sliced**
6   **tablespoons butter**
⅓   **cup flour**
⅓   **cup grated Parmesan cheese**
salt and pepper
¼   **teaspoon grated nutmeg**
1   **pound veal cutlets, pounded thin**

¼   **cup olive oil**
2   **cloves garlic, sliced**
½   **cup beef stock or consommé**
½   **cup dry Madeira**
1   **lemon, thinly sliced**
¼   **cup finely chopped parsley**

- Sauté mushrooms in 2 tablespoons butter about 10 minutes. Set aside.
- Combine flour, cheese and seasonings.
- Dredge veal cutlets in mixture, pressing the mixture into the meat with hands.
- In a skillet large enough to hold the veal in 1 layer, heat remaining butter and oil. Add garlic, then the veal, browning it lightly on both sides (about 3 minutes).
- Pour in stock and Madeira. Bring to a boil, cover and simmer 15 minutes. Add mushrooms and cook 5 minutes longer.
- Garnish with lemon slices and chopped parsley.

Note: Can be browned ahead of time and refrigerated. At the last minute, simmer in stock and wine.

Lemon Veal Scallopine

Light and appealing. Make early in the day for evening company.

Planning:
Can be made ahead

Preparation Time:
15 minutes

Cooking Time:
30 minutes

Yield:
6 to 8 servings

2 pounds veal cutlets
½ cup all-purpose flour
1 to 2 cloves of garlic, pressed
⅓ cup butter
6 lemon slices

1 beef bouillon cube
½ cup hot water
2 tablespoons lemon juice
2 tablespoons chopped fresh parsley

- Preheat oven to 350°.
- Pound veal with mallet to tenderize.
- Stir together flour and garlic. Coat meat with flour mixture.
- Melt butter in a large skillet and brown meat over medium heat about five minutes on each side.
- Place meat in an ungreased 13 x 9-inch baking dish. Top with lemon slices, cover with foil and refrigerate.*
- Dissolve bouillon in water and add lemon juice. Pour over meat and sprinkle with parsley.
- Cover and bake for 25 to 30 minutes.

*Can be made up to this point the day before.

Veal a la Sophie

A dinner party favorite

Planning:
Must marinate two hours;
can be made ahead. Easy to
double.

Preparation Time:
15 minutes

Cooking Time:
25 minutes

Yield:
4 servings

1 **pound boneless veal cutlets**	1 **cup sliced onions**
1 **teaspoon brown bouquet sauce**	1 **3-ounce can sliced mushrooms**
1 **teaspoon salt**	½ **cup sour cream**
1 **teaspoon dry mustard**	2 **tablespoons ketchup**
⅛ **teaspoon pepper**	½ **teaspoon Worcestershire sauce**
⅛ **teaspoon dried marjoram**	**noodles**
3 **tablespoons oil**	

- Pound veal and cut into strips. Mix brown bouquet sauce, salt, mustard, pepper and marjoram in bowl. Coat veal strips. Marinate for two hours.
- Brown veal in oil in a large frying pan. Add onions and simmer five minutes.
- Add mushrooms with liquid. Cover and cook over low heat for 15 minutes. *
- Add sour cream, ketchup and Worcestershire sauce to skillet and heat thoroughly.
- Serve over noodles.

*Can be made ahead to this point.

Veal Scallopine a la Marsala

A colorful version of an old favorite

Preparation Time:
15 minutes

Cooking Time:
15 minutes

Yield:
6 servings

2	pounds veal cutlets
flour	
6	tablespoons sweet butter
2	tablespoons olive oil
4	slices Italian ham (cappicola), diced
1	clove garlic, finely minced
1	teaspoon crumbled dried rosemary

½	teaspoon salt
¼	teaspoon pepper
6	tablespoons Marsala or sherry
2	cups tiny French peas, drained (1 pound can)
¼	cup fresh chopped parsley

- Pound cutlets until thin and dredge in flour.
- Heat butter and olive oil in large skillet. Add veal and ham and sauté 3 minutes in batches, adding more butter and oil if necessary.
- Return to skillet and add the garlic, rosemary, salt and pepper. Cook for 2 minutes.
- Add the wine. Cover and sauté for 3 minutes.
- Uncover. Add the peas and parsley and cook over low heat for 6 minutes longer.

Planning:
Marinate 24 hours

Preparation Time:
5 minutes

Cooking Time:
2 hours

Yield:
6 to 8 servings

Veal Roast

A savory and impressive main course

MARINADE:
1 teaspoon dried basil
1 teaspoon dried parsley
1 teaspoon thyme
2 tablespoons chopped scallions
1 teaspoon salt
1 crushed bay leaf

1 3-ounce can sliced mushrooms, drained
4 tablespoons olive oil
½ teaspoon pepper
1 tablespoon brown bouquet sauce

VEAL:
2 to 3 pound veal roast, boned and rolled
1 tablespoon butter

1 tablespoon flour
1 tablespoon vinegar

- Combine all ingredients for Marinade in bowl large enough to hold roast. Add roast and refrigerate for 24 hours.
- Preheat oven to 350°.
- Remove veal and marinade from bowl. Wrap veal and marinade in foil and seal well. Roast for two hours.
- When the veal is tender, unwrap and pour juices and marinade into a saucepan. Mix in butter, flour and vinegar. Bring to a boil, stirring constantly.
- Serve veal thinly sliced with hot herb mixture.

Veal Marengo

An easy recipe designed to be prepared ahead and frozen. The lemon peel imparts the taste which sets this dish apart from others.

Planning:
Can be frozen

Preparation Time:
30 minutes

Cooking Time:
1 hour

Yield:
8 to 10 servings

4 pounds boneless stewing veal, cubed into bite-sized pieces
3 tablespoons oil
4 tablespoons butter
2 large onions, finely chopped
2 cloves garlic, crushed
3 tablespoons flour
1 cup dry white wine
1½ cups chicken stock

1 16-ounce can peeled tomatoes
2 tablespoons tomato paste
salt and pepper to taste
1 strip of lemon peel
bouquet garni *
1 pound mushrooms, sliced
parsley
1 6-ounce can pitted olives, drained (optional)

- Preheat oven to 350°.
- Brown veal in oil in large frying pan.
- Drain and place veal in a large casserole dish.
- Melt 3 tablespoons butter and sauté onion and garlic until soft. Stir in flour and cook 2 minutes.
- Add wine, stock, tomatoes, tomato paste, salt and pepper. Stir and cook until thickened. Pour over veal.
- Add strip of lemon peel and bouquet garni to casserole. Cover and cook in oven for 1 hour.
- Remove lemon peel and bouquet garni.
- Heat remaining butter and sauté mushrooms for 3 minutes. Stir mushrooms into veal.
- Adjust seasonings, if necessary. Garnish with parsley.

Note: May be garnished at serving time with 1   6-ounce can pitted black olives, drained.

To reheat: heat thawed Veal Maregno in a 325° oven for 30 minutes.

*See Herb Primer page 33.

Preparation Time:
10 minutes

Cooking Time:
20 minutes

Yield:
3 to 4 servings

Pork with Cream and Capers

An elegant approach

2	shallots		salt and pepper
2	tablespoons butter	½	cup chicken stock
1¼	pounds pork cutlets (approximately 6 medium cutlets)	½	cup heavy cream
		2	tablespoons capers

- Mince shallots.
- Melt butter in a large frying pan. Season pork with salt and pepper and sauté over medium heat, turning once (about five minutes). Transfer meat to plate.
- Add chicken stock to pan and deglaze* bottom of pan.
- Add shallots and cook over high heat, stirring often until liquid is thickened, about 10 minutes.
- Stir in heavy cream and return meat to pan along with any juices. Cook over low heat to warm them (about five minutes).
- Add capers and season with salt and pepper.

*Deglaze pan by stirring sides and bottom of pan to gather all accumulated drippings.

Pork Chops with Gruyere

Preparation Time:
10 minutes

Cooking Time:
30 minutes

Yield:
4 servings

The richness of the cheese is a perfect complement to the pork. This is an easy way to dress up chops.

4	loin pork chops (about 1½ pounds)	1	tablespoon Dijon mustard
salt		1	tablespoon heavy cream
pepper		½	teaspoon finely chopped garlic
1	tablespoon peanut oil	1	egg yolk
¼	pound grated Gruyere cheese (approximately one cup)	1	tablespoon finely chopped chives

- Sprinkle the chops with salt and pepper to taste.
- Heat the oil in a heavy skillet and add the chops. Cook until nicely browned on one side (about ten minutes) and continue cooking until browned on the other side and cooked through.
- Preheat the broiler.
- As the chops cook, blend the cheese, mustard, cream, garlic, egg yolk and chives.
- When the chops are cooked, spread one side with the cheese mixture.
- Put under broiler until topping is browned and glazed.

Preparation Time:
10 minutes

Cooking Time:
2½ to 3 hours

Yield:
8 servings

Cherry Almond Pork Roast

A holiday favorite

1 **4-pound pork loin roast, boned, rolled and tied**
salt
pepper
⅓ **cup slivered almonds**
1 **12-ounce jar all fruit cherry preserves**

3 **tablespoons light corn syrup**
⅓ **cup red wine vinegar**
¼ **teaspoon ground cloves**
¼ **teaspoon ground cinnamon**
¼ **teaspoon ground nutmeg**

- Preheat oven to 325°.
- Rub roast with salt and pepper and place in uncovered roasting pan. Roast for 2 to 2½ hours.
- Toast the almonds in a dry skillet, stirring often to avoid burning and reserve.
- In a small saucepan, mix remaining ingredients. Bring to a boil, stirring frequently. Reduce heat and simmer a few minutes. Add almonds and keep sauce warm.
- Baste roast several times with sauce while roasting for thirty minutes more or until the meat thermometer reaches 170°.
- Serve remaining sauce with roast.

Note: Black cherry, apricot preserves or orange marmalade can be substituted for the cherry preserves in this recipe. Also great used as a ham glaze.

Pork Chops with Orange

Family fare at its best!

Preparation Time:
10 minutes

Cooking Time:
35 minutes

Yield:
4 servings

4   loin pork chops, boneless
salt and freshly ground pepper
3   tablespoons butter
2   large seedless navel oranges
½   cup finely chopped onion

1½   tablespoons lemon juice
1   cup canned chicken broth
1   tablespoon tomato paste
½   teaspoon grated orange peel
½   teaspoon sugar

- Sprinkle chops with salt and pepper.
- Heat two tablespoons butter in very hot skillet and add chops. Cook over moderately high heat uncovered until nicely browned and turn. Keep turning and cooking for about 30 minutes to make sure pork is thoroughly cooked but not dry.
- Trim off end of oranges and cut unpeeled oranges into eight rounds. Set aside.
- Remove chops to warming rack in oven and pour off fat from skillet. To skillet add the onion and cook until wilted. Add juice of lemon and stir. Add broth, tomato paste and grated orange peel and stir to blend, cooking gently. Add sugar, salt and pepper to taste.
- After five minutes cooking, add orange slices and any juices from the pork chops. Cook, turning slices, about three minutes.
- Arrange orange slices over pork chops. Swirl one tablespoon butter into gravy and serve it separately.

POULTRY

Turkey and Wild Rice Casserole

This is a perfect recipe for a large gathering.

Planning:
Soak rice for 1 hour. Can be made ahead of time and heated before serving.

Preparation Time:
5 minutes plus 15 minutes

Cooking Time:
1½ hours

Yield:
10 to 12 servings

1   **cup wild rice**
1   **pound mushrooms, sliced**
½   **cup chopped onion**
6   **tablespoons butter**
3   **cups diced cooked turkey or chicken**

¼   **teaspoon pepper**
½   **cup sliced almonds**
3   **cups chicken broth**
1½   **cups heavy cream**

- Wash rice. Cover with water and bring to boiling. Remove from heat and let soak 1 hour. Drain.
- Preheat oven to 350°.
- Sauté mushrooms and onion in 3 tablespoons of butter until browned. Combine mushroom mixture with rice, turkey or chicken, pepper, almonds, broth and cream.
- Mix together and turn into a buttered casserole dish. Cover and bake for 1¼ hours.
- Remove cover. Dot with remaining butter. Bake 15 to 20 minutes.

Note: Easy to double. Chicken works as well as turkey.

Chicken Bolognese

Perfect for a group luncheon or dinner

Planning:
Can flour and brown chicken ahead of time

Preparation Time:
15 minutes

Cooking Time:
25 minutes

Yield:
4 to 6 servings

8   **chicken breasts, halved, skinned and boned**
salt
freshly ground black pepper
flour
3   **tablespoons butter**
2   **tablespoons oil**
8   **thin slices prosciutto**

8   **thin slices fontina or bel paese cheese**
4   **teaspoons freshly grated Parmesan cheese**
2   **tablespoons chicken stock, fresh or canned (white wine can be substituted)**

- Preheat oven to 350°.
- Pound chicken breasts between two sheets of waxed paper to flatten. Strip off paper.
- Season breasts with salt and a few grindings of pepper. Dredge in flour, shake off excess.
- In a heavy 10- to 12-inch skillet, melt butter with oil over moderate heat. Brown chicken to a light golden color, 3 to 4 pieces at a time.
- Transfer chicken to a shallow buttered baking and serving dish.
- Place a slice of prosciutto and a slice of cheese on each piece. Sprinkle with grated cheese and drizzle chicken stock over them.
- Bake uncovered in the middle of the oven for 10 minutes or until cheese is melted and lightly browned. Serve at once.

Summer Spinach-Stuffed Chicken

Light & tasty. This main course travels easily.

Planning:
Make ahead and serve at room temperature

Preparation Time:
20 minutes

Cooking Time:
20 minutes

Yield:
6 to 8 servings

8	slices bacon
1	large onion, finely chopped
2	cloves garlic, crushed
1	10-ounce package frozen spinach, thawed and squeezed dry
1	cup crushed seasoned croutons
4	eggs
4	whole chicken breasts, halved, skinned and boned
1½	cups bread crumbs
1	teaspoon salt
1	teaspoon pepper
6	tablespoons oil

- In a medium-sized skillet, fry bacon until crisp. Drain, reserving 2 tablespoons drippings and set aside.
- Sauté onion and garlic in drippings until soft. Remove from heat.
- Crumble bacon and stir into skillet along with spinach and croutons. Lightly beat 2 eggs and stir into mixture.
- Lightly pound each chicken breast until flat. With sharp knife, cut a pocket in thick side of each breast.
- Divide spinach mixture into 8 equal parts. Stuff each breast with mixture and secure with a toothpick.
- Lightly beat 2 remaining eggs. Mix together bread crumbs, salt and pepper.
- Dip each cutlet into eggs and coat with crumbs.
- Heat oil in large skillet over medium-low heat. (A non-stick skillet is best.) Add cutlets and cover pan. Cook over low heat for 10 minutes. Turn cutlets over and cook for 7 minutes.
- Remove from skillet. Let cool and remove toothpicks. Serve at room temperature.

Note: Easy to halve or double.

Toothpicks on hand make preparing this recipe a snap.

Preparation Time:
30 minutes

Cooking Time:
20 minutes

Yield:
4 servings

Curried Stuffed Chicken Breasts

This will be a popular menu choice.

3 tablespoons butter
½ cup finely chopped onion
½ cup finely chopped celery
¼ teaspoon finely minced garlic
1 bay leaf
1 cup apple, peeled, cored and cut into small (¼-inch) cubes
3 tablespoons white seedless raisins (soaked in warm water to plump)

3 tablespoons chutney
2 large whole, boned chicken breasts, halved (4 pieces)
salt and pepper to taste
½ cup heavy cream
1 teaspoon curry powder

- Preheat oven to 425°.
- Heat 1 tablespoon of the butter in a large skillet and sauté onion, celery, garlic and bay leaf. When onion wilts, add the apple, stirring over medium heat for 2 minutes. Add chopped raisins (squeeze liquid from them before chopping) and chutney. Stir and remove from heat. Let cool.
- Place chicken breasts skin-side down and pound lightly. Sprinkle with salt and pepper. Place equal portions of filling in middle and fold edges to make a package. Secure edges with toothpicks.
- Melt remaining 2 tablespoons of butter in a shallow baking dish. Place chicken breast packages, seam-side down in dish, and cook on top of stove for 1 minute. Bake for 10 minutes. Baste once.
- Blend cream and curry powder in a small bowl. Pour over breasts. Bake 10 more minutes.

Chicken Annabella

Preparation Time:
20 minutes

Cooking Time:
1 hour and 10 minutes

Yield:
8 to 10 servings

Remarkable combination of flavors. Make ahead to serve hot or at room temperature.

flour, for dredging
3 pounds chicken breasts, skinned and boned, cut into stew-size pieces
¼ cup olive oil, for browning chicken
1 *head* of garlic, peeled and finely minced
¼ cup dried oregano
salt and pepper to taste
½ cup red wine vinegar

½ cup olive oil (additional)
1 cup pitted and coarsely chopped prunes
½ cup pitted Spanish olives (optional)
½ cup capers with a bit of liquid
6 bay leaves
1 cup brown sugar
2 cups white wine
chicken broth — if needed

- Preheat oven to 350°.
- Place flour in plastic bag. Add chicken in 2 to 3 batches to coat pieces.
- Heat 2 tablespoons olive oil in large skillet and sauté half of chicken until nicely browned. Remove with slotted spoon. Brown remaining chicken in additional 2 tablespoons of oil.
- Place browned chicken in oven-proof pot or casserole. Mix in garlic, oregano, salt and pepper, vinegar, olive oil, prunes, Spanish olives, capers, bay leaves, brown sugar and white wine.
- Bake, covered, for 1 hour and 10 minutes, stirring occasionally. Sauce will thicken. Add more wine, water or chicken broth, if necessary.

Note: Serve with rice.

Preparation Time:
20 minutes

Cooking Time:
20 minutes

Yield:
4 servings

Pecan Breaded Chicken

This is so good you could serve it alone.

2 **whole chicken breasts, halved, skinned and boned**
6 **tablespoons butter or margarine**
3 **tablespoons Dijon mustard, divided use**

5 to 6 ounces pecans
safflower oil for greasing baking pan
⅔ **cup sour cream**
salt to taste
freshly ground pepper

- Preheat oven to 400°.
- Slightly pound chicken breasts. Place chicken between two pieces of waxed paper and lightly flatten with a bottle.
- Melt butter in a small saucepan over medium heat. Remove from heat and whisk in 2 tablespoons mustard.
- Coarsely grind pecans in food processor.
- Dip each chicken piece in the mustard mixture, then heavily coat with ground pecans.
- Place in oiled baking dish and bake for 20 minutes.
- While chicken is baking, combine sour cream and 1 tablespoon of mustard in a small skillet. Add salt and pepper to taste. Quickly bring to a boil and remove from heat.
- To serve, place cream sauce on individual plates and then place chicken breast on top.

Three Spice Chicken with Mushrooms

A contemporary approach to chicken

Preparation Time:
15 minutes

Cooking Time:
35 minutes

Yield:
2 to 4 servings

2   whole chicken breasts, halved, skinned and boned (4 pieces)
freshly ground pepper
flour for dredging
3   tablespoons olive oil
8   cloves garlic, peeled
1   pound mushrooms (if large, halve them)

¼   cup chopped fresh basil
4   tablespoons balsamic vinegar
¾   cup chicken broth (more if needed)
1   bay leaf
¼   teaspoon dried thyme

- Season chicken pieces generously with fresh ground pepper and dredge in flour, shaking off any excess.
- Heat oil in a large skillet. Add chicken and cook over medium-high heat until golden brown on one side (about 3 minutes). Add garlic.
- Turn chicken to other side and add mushrooms and basil. Shake pan so mushrooms cook evenly for about 3 minutes.
- Add vinegar, broth, bay leaf and thyme to skillet. Cover and cook over medium-low heat for 10 minutes, turning chicken a few times.
- Place chicken on warm platter. Cook mushrooms and sauce over medium-heat uncovered for 5 minutes.
- Remove bay leaf and pour sauce and mushrooms over chicken.

grace huntley pugh ©

LARCHMONT MANOR PARK

It is nearly synonymous with the village whose coastline it hugs. Here children clamber among glacier-strewn rocks, one acknowledged generation after generation as the "dinosaur egg". On the first real day of spring, high school students sprout like dandelions bringing with them guitars and Frisbees. As Easter dawns, neighbors worship together here. During Race Week, sailing enthusiasts man the sea wall, following the Lightnings as they make their first turn off Prospect Point.

In Manor Park, we pose for our wedding portraits, walk our dogs and toddlers, and watch the seasons change from green to gold to silver.

Last Minute Company Chicken Kiev

Preparation Time:
15 minutes

Cooking Time:
45 minutes

Yield:
4 servings

Raves from all!

½ cup bread crumbs
2 tablespoons grated
Parmesan cheese
1 teaspoon basil
1 teaspoon oregano
¼ teaspoon salt
2 whole chicken breasts,
halved and boned

⅔ cup butter, melted
2 cloves garlic, pressed
¼ cup white wine
¼ cup chopped scallions
¼ cup chopped fresh parsley

- Preheat oven to 350°.
- Mix bread crumbs, cheese, basil, oregano and salt. Dip chicken in melted butter, then crumb mixture. Place in a buttered casserole dish.
- Bake 45 minutes or until golden.
- While chicken is cooking, sauté garlic in remaining butter using a small skillet. Then add wine, scallions and parsley. Pour sauce over chicken. Bake another 3 to 5 minutes until sauce is hot. Serve at once.

Preparation Time:
10 minutes

Cooking Time:
50 minutes

Yield:
2 to 4 servings

Parmesan Yogurt Chicken

*Easy and inexpensive with
a gourmet appearance*

1   3-pound broiler-fryer chicken, cut up
2   tablespoons lemon juice
salt and pepper to taste
½   cup plain yogurt
¼   cup mayonnaise
1   tablespoon Dijon mustard

1   tablespoon Worcestershire sauce
½   teaspoon thyme
¼   teaspoon cayenne pepper
¼   cup thinly sliced scallions
½   cup grated Parmesan cheese

- Preheat oven to 350°.
- Arrange chicken pieces skin-side up in baking dish. Cover with lemon juice, salt and pepper.
- Thoroughly blend yogurt, mayonnaise, mustard, Worcestershire sauce, thyme, cayenne and scallions. Spread mixture evenly over chicken.
- Bake uncovered for 50 minutes.
- Remove from oven and carefully drain off pan juices.
- Sprinkle chicken with Parmesan cheese and broil about 4 inches from heat until cheese melts and browns slightly, about 3 minutes. Serve immediately.

Baked Chicken with Currant Sauce

The spiced fruity sauce is a snap to make.

Planning:
Can be dredged earlier in day — then brought to room temperature and baked prior to serving

Preparation Time:
Chicken, 10 minutes
Sauce, 5 minutes

Cooking Time:
Chicken, 30 minutes
Sauce, 15 to 20 minutes

Yield:
8 servings

CHICKEN:

2	cups seasoned bread crumbs	4	whole chicken breasts, halved, skinned and boned
2	tablespoons sesame seeds	½	cup butter, melted

SAUCE:

1	cup red currant jelly	1	teaspoon dry mustard
1	6-ounce can frozen orange juice concentrate, thawed	⅛	teaspoon ground ginger
4	tablespoons dry sherry	¼	teaspoon hot pepper sauce

- Preheat oven to 350°.
- On a plate, combine bread crumbs and sesame seeds. Dip chicken in melted butter and then in crumb mixture. Place in buttered baking dish. Bake for 30 minutes.
- While chicken is baking, combine all sauce ingredients in a medium pan and simmer until smooth. Serve sauce on side.

Planning:
Can be coated ahead of time

Preparation Time:
20 minutes

Cooking Time:
25 minutes

Yield:
6 servings

Chicken Oporto

Fits the bill for an easy company dish

½ cup butter
½ pound mushrooms, thinly sliced
¼ cup flour
¼ teaspoon pepper
salt to taste
¼ teaspoon ground nutmeg

4 medium whole chicken breasts, halved, skinned and boned
1½ cups light cream
⅓ cup white port wine or dry sherry

- Melt butter over medium heat using a 12-inch skillet. Add mushrooms and cook for 5 minutes. Remove mushrooms with slotted spoon and set aside.
- Combine flour, pepper, salt and nutmeg. Coat chicken breasts with mixture. Add chicken to butter remaining in skillet and brown. Stir in cream, port and mushrooms. Heat until boiling.
- Reduce heat to low, cover and simmer for 15 minutes.
- Serve with sauce.

Chicken Paprika

A classic

Preparation Time:
15 minutes

Cooking Time:
20 minutes

Yield:
4 servings

2 pounds chicken cutlets	1 teaspoon paprika
1 egg, beaten	1 10-ounce can chicken broth
flour, for dredging	½ pound mushrooms, sliced
4 tablespoons olive oil	1½ teaspoons flour
1 cup coarsely chopped onion	1 8-ounce carton sour cream

- Dip chicken cutlets in egg and then flour. Brown cutlets in large skillet with olive oil. Remove from skillet with slotted spoon.

- In the same pan, sauté onions. When tender, but not brown, remove from heat and stir in paprika. Mix well.

- Return chicken to skillet, add broth and mushrooms. Cover and simmer 20 minutes. Remove to heated dish.

- In a small bowl, blend 1½ teaspoons flour and sour cream well. Bring liquid in frying pan to a simmer, then add sour cream mixture. Stir constantly over low heat and avoid boiling. (A light simmer will thicken the sauce sufficiently.) Pour over chicken cutlets and serve.

Preparation Time:
15 minutes

Cooking Time:
45 minutes to 1 hour

Yield:
4 servings

Chicken Baltino

An Italian dish to be served with pasta

1 head garlic, pressed	½ 6-ounce can black olives, drained and sliced
1 cup sliced fresh mushrooms	1 or 2 6½-ounce jars artichoke hearts, partially drained and cut in half
1 cup chopped scallions	
3 tablespoons fresh basil	
½ cup olive oil	1 cup dry red wine
2 whole chicken breasts, halved, skinned and boned	¼ cup grated Parmesan cheese
1 14½-ounce can Italian style tomatoes with juice	

- In large skillet, sauté garlic, mushrooms, scallions and basil in olive oil.
- Pound chicken breasts to desired thinness.
- Add chicken, tomatoes with juice, olives, artichoke hearts and red wine to skillet. Simmer covered for 20 minutes or until chicken is cooked.
- Sprinkle with Parmesan cheese.

Note: If thicker sauce is desired, gradually add 1 to 2 tablespoons of cornstarch or flour.

Perfect with angel hair or vermicelli.

Chicken Yakitori

Always a favorite as served by Japanese families at our school fairs.

Planning:
Sauce can be made ahead of time. Can keep for approximately nine months in refrigerator.

Preparation Time:
25 minutes

Cooking Time:
15 minutes for the sauce
30 minutes for the chicken

Yield:
8 servings

8 wooden skewers
4 whole chicken breasts, halved, skinned and boned
3 cups soy sauce
3 cups sake (a Japanese wine)

2 cups sugar
pressed garlic to taste
minced fresh ginger to taste
4 green peppers, cut in bite-sized chunks

- Preheat oven to 350°. Also, start grill if using.*
- Soak wooden skewers in water.
- Cut chicken into bite-sized pieces.
- Bake chicken for 5 to 10 minutes (until half-cooked) in an ungreased 9x13x2-inch pan.
- While chicken is cooking, combine soy sauce, sake and sugar in a large saucepan. Bring to a boil, then simmer until the liquid is reduced to ⅔ of the original amount. Add garlic and ginger to the sauce. Refrigerate if not using immediately.
- Alternate peppers and chicken pieces on soaked wooden skewers.
- Dip skewers in the sauce and grill chicken until it is thoroughly cooked. Baste with remaining sauce while grilling.

Note: This recipe is easily cut in half, but keep some sauce on hand for summer barbecues.

*Skewers can also be placed under oven broiler.

Planning:
Can be made ahead

Preparation Time:
15 minutes

Cooking Time:
45 to 50 minutes

Yield:
4 to 6 servings

Finger Lickin' Picnic Chicken

Sure to become a family favorite

8	chicken legs	1	cup sour cream or plain yogurt
8	chicken thighs		
salt and pepper		2	cups packaged cornflake crumbs
1	cup Dijon or spicy mustard		

- Preheat oven to 400°.

- Salt and pepper chicken pieces.

- In a bowl, mix together mustard and sour cream or yogurt. Dip each chicken piece in mixture, lightly covering. Then dip pieces in cornflake crumbs. (Crumbs can be put in plastic bag for easy clean-up.)

- Place pieces in an ungreased baking dish. Make a foil tent to cover. Bake for 30 minutes.

- Remove foil tent and bake an additional 15 to 20 minutes at 450°.

- Serve hot, at room temperature or cooled for picnic.

Baked Mustard Chicken

Tender and yummy

Preparation Time:
5 minutes

Cooking Time:
45 to 50 minutes

Yield:
4 servings

4 chicken breast halves, skinned and boned
¼ cup spicy brown mustard
½ cup toasted flavored bread crumbs
¼ cup butter or margarine, melted
2 tablespoons lemon juice
2 tablespoons water or white wine
paprika

- Preheat oven to 350°.
- Brush chicken with mustard and dredge in bread crumbs. Place in a 9x13x2-inch baking dish breast-side up.
- Combine butter, lemon juice and water. Drizzle 1 tablespoon over each piece of chicken and pour remainder in dish.
- Cover and bake for 30 minutes. Remove cover, sprinkle with paprika and bake an additional 15 to 20 minutes.

Preparation Time:
20 minutes

Cooking Time:
30 to 40 minutes

Yield:
8 servings

Chicken Dijon

*Pretty when garnished with
red grapes and watercress.*

4	whole chicken breasts, halved, skinned and boned	2	tablespoons oil
¼	cup flour, plus 1½ tablespoons	1½	tablespoons all-purpose flour
	salt to taste (approximately 1 teaspoon)	2	tablespoons Dijon mustard
		¾	cup milk
¼	teaspoon pepper	⅓	cup white wine
3½	tablespoons butter, divided use	¼	teaspoon dried tarragon

- Preheat oven to 325°.
- Dredge chicken in ¼ cup flour, salt and pepper. In frying pan, sauté chicken in 2 tablespoons butter and oil, turning once until golden. Arrange in casserole.
- Melt 1½ tablespoons butter in saucepan. Whisk in flour and mustard, stirring constantly until bubbly. Whisk in milk, wine and tarragon. Cook until mixture thickens and bubbles for one minute. Pour sauce over chicken.
- Bake covered for 30 to 40 minutes. Arrange chicken on platter and spoon sauce over top.

Braised Chicken Breasts

Preparation Time:
15 minutes

Cooking Time:
40 minutes

Yield:
4 to 6 servings

*Fresh asparagus and French bread
will complete this meal.*

6	chicken cutlets	½	cup water
2	tablespoons flour	1	teaspoon prepared
1	tablespoon olive oil		mustard
3	tablespoons butter or	½	teaspoon salt
	margarine	⅛	teaspoon pepper
1	small onion, diced	¼	cup heavy cream
1	8-ounce can stewed		
	tomatoes		

- Coat chicken cutlets with flour. In a 12-inch skillet over medium-high heat, heat olive oil and butter or margarine until melted. Add chicken and onion. Cook until chicken is browned on all sides and onion is tender.

- Stir in tomatoes with liquid, water, mustard, salt and pepper over high heat. Heat to boiling. Reduce heat to low. Cover and simmer 25 minutes or until chicken is tender.

- When chicken is done, skim off fat from liquid, and stir in heavy cream. Cook until heated through.

Chicken Breasts Piquant

Planning:
Refrigerate 4 to 6 hours prior to baking

Preparation Time:
10 minutes

Cooking Time:
45 minutes

Yield:
6 servings

*Perfect to start at lunchtime —
then heat up for supper*

3	whole chicken breasts, halved and boned or 2½ to 3 pounds cut-up chicken
1½	cups Rosé or dry red wine
½	cup soy sauce
¼	cup olive or salad oil
4	tablespoons water
2	cloves garlic, sliced
2	teaspoons ginger
½	teaspoon oregano
2	tablespoons brown sugar
	fresh parsley

- Place chicken pieces in a casserole.
- Combine Rosé or red wine, soy sauce, oil, water, garlic, ginger, oregano and brown sugar. Pour marinade over chicken and refrigerate 4 to 6 hours.
- Preheat oven to 375°.
- Remove from refrigerator and bring to room temperature. Cover and bake in marinade for 45 minutes or until heated through.
- Garnish with parsley.

Note: Serve on a bed of rice.

Roast Chicken with Cracked Peppercorn Sauce

Preparation Time:
20 minutes

Cooking Time:
20 minutes per pound

Yield:
4 servings

Makes a simple meal elegant

1   broiler-fryer chicken (4 to 5 pounds)
salt and pepper
1½   cups vermouth
4   shallots, chopped

1   garlic clove, minced
1   cup heavy cream, hot
1   tablespoon cracked* black peppercorns

- Preheat oven to 350°.
- Remove giblets and season chicken inside and out with salt and pepper.**
- Roast chicken in pan with vermouth, shallots and garlic in oven.
- Strain cooking liquid into a saucepan and reduce it to ½ cup over high heat.
- Stir in hot cream and cracked peppercorns. Cook for 5 minutes.
- Serve over carved chicken.

*Use the bottom of a heavy skillet to crack the peppercorns (or look for them in your grocer's spice section).

**Chicken can be stuffed with your favorite stuffing.

SEAFOOD

Mussels Marseille

Try this for its delicate flavor.

Preparation Time:
15 minutes

Cooking Time:
10 minutes

Yield:
4 servings

4 **dozen mussels**	3 **tablespoons finely**
2 **tablespoons butter**	**chopped parsley**
3 **shallots**	¾ **cup heavy cream**
6 **ounces clam juice**	**salt and freshly ground pepper**
1 **cup white wine**	**juice of ½ lemon or to taste**

- Clean mussels and debeard. Place in Dutch oven with butter, shallots, clam juice, white wine and parsley.
- Steam, covered, until mussels open, about 7 minutes.
- Add remaining ingredients and return to boil and serve.

Planning:
Can be made ahead

Preparation Time:
20 minutes

Cooking Time:
20 to 30 minutes

Yield:
3 to 4 servings

Scallops in Wine Sauce

Rich in flavor and taste

---

1 **pound scallops, cut if large**	1 **tablespoon chopped**
1 **cup dry white wine**	**parsley**
1¼ **tablespoons lemon juice**	3 **tablespoons butter**
¼ **pound fresh mushrooms,**	1 **tablespoon flour**
sliced or 1 3-ounce can,	2 **tablespoons heavy cream**
drained	**salt and pepper to taste**
4 **shallots, finely chopped**	2 **tablespoons bread crumbs**

- Preheat broiler or preheat oven to 350°.
- Place scallops, wine and lemon juice in a shallow pan. Cover and simmer 5 to 10 minutes until scallops are tender. Remove scallops, save liquid.
- Using the same pan, sauté mushrooms, shallots and parsley in butter for 3 to 5 minutes.
- Stir in flour and then blend in reserved liquid and cream. Bring to a boil, stirring. Season to taste with salt and pepper.
- Add scallops to sauce and pour into greased shallow baking dish or individual shells.
- Sprinkle with bread crumbs.
- Place under preheated broiler until lightly browned *or* bake for 15 to 20 minutes until bubbling.

Scallops with Fresh Ginger

Preparation Time:
15 minutes

Cooking Time:
6 to 8 minutes

Yield:
4 servings

A great dish for entertaining since everything can be prepared in advance and cooked up in 6 to 8 minutes.

10 tablespoons butter
2 tablespoons finely chopped shallots
1 cup julienne carrots
2 tablespoons finely chopped ginger
½ cup dry white wine

½ cup heavy cream
salt and pepper to taste
1¼ pounds bay scallops
1 cup julienne zucchini
¾ cup shredded leeks (optional)

- Heat 2 tablespoons of the butter. Add shallots and cook briefly.
- Stir in carrots and cook about 45 seconds.
- Stir in ginger.
- Add wine and reduce almost completely.
- Add cream, salt and pepper. Cook down over high heat until sauce is reduced by half.
- Add scallops, zucchini and leeks. Cook stirring about 1½ minutes and swirl in remaining butter.
- Serve with rice.

Preparation Time:
15 minutes

Cooking Time:
15 to 20 minutes

Yield:
2 to 4 servings

Scallop Sauté

Zingy

1½ pounds scallops (bay are preferable to ocean — if using ocean, cut large scallops in half)
2 tablespoons butter

½ cup tarragon vinegar
½ cup heavy cream
1 tablespoon Dijon mustard
salt and pepper to taste
parsley, chopped

- Sauté scallops in a large frying pan using butter until almost cooked (approximately two minutes).
- Remove scallops and keep warm. Also remove pan juices and save.
- Add vinegar to the frying pan and cook over high heat until the vinegar is reduced to 2 tablespoons.
- Add pan juices and heavy cream to the vinegar and cook over medium high heat until sauce is thick.
- Add mustard to mixture and season with salt and pepper.
- Add scallops to briefly reheat. Serve immediately.
- Sprinkle parsley over each serving.

Shrimp Casserole

Sunday night shrimp

Planning:
Can be prepared earlier in day

Preparation Time:
40 minutes

Cooking Time:
20 minutes.

Yield:
4 servings

¼ **cup chopped onion**
2 **tablespoons butter**
2 **tablespoons flour**
½ **teaspoon salt**
dash of pepper
1 **cup light cream**
½ **teaspoon Worcestershire sauce**
1 **3-ounce can sliced mushrooms, drained**

2 **cups cleaned shrimp (1 pound)**
2 **cups hot cooked rice**
½ **cup shredded Cheddar cheese**
½ **cup cracker crumbs**
parsley

- Preheat oven to 350°.
- In large Dutch oven, cook onion in butter until tender. Blend in flour, salt and pepper. Gradually add cream and Worcestershire sauce. Cook and stir until thick.
- Add mushrooms and shrimp. Cook until heated through.
- Place rice in a greased casserole.
- Place shrimp mixture on top of rice and top with cheese and crumbs.
- Bake uncovered for 20 minutes.
- Garnish with parsley.

Barbecued Shrimp

Preparation Time:
10 minutes

Cooking Time:
5 to 7 minutes

Yield:
4 to 6 servings

For that great Cajun flavor

2   pounds large shrimp,
    peeled
1¼ tablespoons minced garlic
2   teaspoons Creole
    Seasoning*
1½ teaspoons dried rosemary

¾   cup beer
2   tablespoons
    Worcestershire sauce
¾   cup butter or margarine,
    softened

- Heat large skillet over high heat until hot. Add shrimp, garlic, Creole Seasoning and rosemary. Sauté shrimp 1 minute, shaking skillet.
- Add beer and Worcestershire sauce. Simmer 2 minutes. Lower heat slightly.
- Pick up butter on wire whisk, a tablespoon at a time and whisk into sauce. Heat thoroughly, but do not let mixture boil.
- Stir so that sauce coats shrimp.
- Serve immediately.

*CREOLE SEASONING:
4½ teaspoons salt
4   teaspoons black pepper
2   teaspoons dried thyme
2   teaspoons dried oregano
2   teaspoons dried basil

2   teaspoons paprika
1   teaspoon cayenne pepper
1   teaspoon onion powder
1   teaspoon garlic powder

- In a small bowl combine all ingredients.
- Store in an air-tight jar.

My Mother's Shrimp Creole

A family recipe directly from Louisiana's bayou.

Preparation Time:
30 minutes

Cooking Time:
45 minutes

Yield:
8 servings

¼	cup flour
¼	cup vegetable oil
2	cups chopped onions
1	garlic clove, minced
1	cup chopped green pepper
1	30-ounce can tomato sauce
3	pounds peeled, raw shrimp
1	cup water
1	teaspoon salt

¼	teaspoon black pepper
½	teaspoon hot pepper sauce
2	teaspoons Worcestershire sauce
1½	cups chopped celery
½	cup chopped parsley
¼	cup chopped scallion tops
2	bay leaves
2	thin lemon slices

- In a heavy pot, make a roux by stirring flour and oil together over medium high heat until it turns a caramel color.
- Add onions, garlic and green pepper and sauté until onions are soft.
- Add tomato sauce and simmer for 5 minutes.
- Add peeled, raw shrimp (fresh or rinsed frozen shrimp).
- Add 1 cup water to thin.
- Simmer to blend — do not boil!
- Add remaining ingredients. Cover and simmer for 30 minutes, stirring occasionally.
- Remove bay leaf and lemon.
- Serve over hot, fluffy rice.

Note: Recipe may be halved.

Preparation Time:
20 minutes

Cooking Time:
8 to 10 minutes, plus 10
minutes more

Yield:
4 servings

Shrimp with Feta Cheese

Shrimp — spicy style

5 tablespoons olive oil
4 cloves garlic, finely
   minced
2 cups stewed tomatoes
⅓ cup dry white wine
¼ cup finely chopped basil
1 teaspoon dried oregano
freshly ground pepper to taste
1½ pounds fresh medium
   shrimp, shelled and
   deveined

¼ teaspoon hot red pepper
   flakes
½ pound crumbled feta
   cheese
½ 16-ounce box orzo, cooked
   according to package
   directions

- Preheat oven to 400°.
- Using a large skillet, heat 2 tablespoons oil and briefly cook garlic, about 1 minute.
- Add tomatoes, wine, basil, oregano and freshly ground pepper.
- Cook, stirring, for 5 minutes or until heated through.
- Heat remaining 3 tablespoons oil in another skillet. Add shrimp and sauté briefly, just until pink, stirring often. Sprinkle with pepper flakes.
- Pour shrimp and oil into 2-quart baking dish. Sprinkle with cheese and pour tomato sauce over.
- Bake for 10 minutes, until heated through.
- Meanwhile, cook orzo according to package directions.
- Serve orzo with shrimp along side.

Grilled Seafood Skewers

Ocean melody

Planning:
Must marinate for at least 3 hours

Preparation Time:
15 minutes

Cooking Time:
15 minutes medium-high on a gas grill or hot coals on a charcoal grill

Yield:
2 servings

MARINADE:

2   cloves garlic, minced
½   cup olive oil

2   snips fresh dill (or 1 teaspoon dried)

FOR EACH SKEWER:

2   jumbo shrimp
2   1-inch pieces swordfish
2   large sea scallops
2   small round onions, peeled and parboiled

1   large piece green pepper
1   large piece red pepper
2   cherry tomatoes or 2 quarters of tomato

- At least 3 hours prior to serving mix marinade ingredients. Marinate shrimp, swordfish and sea scallops in the refrigerator.
- Preheat grill.
- Thread long skewers with seafood, onions, green and red pepper and tomatoes.
- Place on grill over hot coals.
- Cover and cook 5 to 7 minutes on one side, basting frequently with marinade.
- Turn, cover and cook an additional 7 minutes, basting frequently.

Note: Serve with rice, corn on the cob and Blueberry Batter Cake for any easy summer menu.

Preparation Time:
10 minutes

Cooking Time:
10 to 15 minutes

Yield:
3 to 4 servings

Salmon with Mustard Sauce

The sauce adds just enough taste not to obscure the fresh fish flavor.

1½ pounds fillet of salmon

SAUCE:

2 **tablespoons salted butter, melted**

2 **teaspoons Dijon mustard**

2 **teaspoons fresh dill (chopped)**

- Preheat barbecue or broiler.
- Blend butter, mustard, and dill in a small bowl.
- Place fillets skin-side down onto a greased baking pan.* Spread ½ of sauce on top of salmon.
- Broil close to heat 6 to 10 minutes, being careful to avoid burning.
- Spread balance of butter sauce on fish just before serving.

*Salmon may be cooked (skin-side down directly on grill) on hot barbecue with top down for 10 to 15 minutes or just until it flakes.

Note: When cooked on the grill the bottom heat makes the skin wonderfully crisp.

Grilled Salmon and Soy Sauce

Marinade and sauce make a delicious difference

Planning:
Marinate 8 hours

Preparation Time:
10 minutes

Cooking Time:
10 to 15 minutes

Yield:
Depends on quantity of salmon

Salmon (fillet, whole or steaks)
soy sauce
cider vinegar

mayonnaise
honey

- Cover salmon with equal parts soy sauce and vinegar. Refrigerate for at least 8 hours.
- When ready to cook salmon, place marinade on stove and reduce by half. Preheat grill or broiler.
- Meanwhile, in a bowl, take mayonnaise and add honey to taste. (Start with 1 tablespoon of honey per cup of mayonnaise. Add more of either if necessary.)
- Add reduced soy marinade to mayonnaise mixture by tablespoons, whisking in as you add. You are looking for a light brown sauce the consistency of yogurt. Additional mayonnaise mix may be required.
- Grill or broil salmon to desired doneness. (For every ½-inch in thickness, cook salmon 5 to 6 minutes. A 1-inch thick steak will require 10 to 12 minutes of cooking time.)
- Pour sauce over salmon or serve on the side.

Note: Last four ingredients have no measurements because quantity of salmon is determining factor.

grace huntley pugh ©

ROBERT E. DERECKTOR, YACHT BUILDERS

Traffic on the Boston Post Road in Mamaroneck occasionally backs up to allow a huge tractor trailer shouldering a brand new, sleek, white yacht out of Derecktor's boatyard and into the stream of shoppers and commuters. Dwarfed in our Toyotas, we wonder where she is bound, what exotic port of call or tranquil bay? On which of the seven seas will her bow splice blue-green waters?

Bob Derecktor has been building and repairing all classes of yachts in Mamaroneck since 1947. And he is the best. Just ask Dennis O'Connor who recaptured the America's Cup in 1987 with Derecktor-built "Stars and Stripes". Bob Derecktor is equally proud of "Grey Goose II", the 72 foot sailing yacht he designed and built for himself. As her skipper, he won the 1989 Nantucket Bucket.

Black Sea Bass St. Augustine

A surprise scrumptious filling!

Planning:
Marinate 1 hour. Let sit 15 minutes after cooking.

Preparation Time:
20 minutes

Cooking Time:
20 to 25 minutes

Yield:
4 to 6 servings

8   fillets (2½ pounds) Black Sea Bass, Sole or Striped Bass, boneless and skinless
salt to taste
¼   cup fresh lemon juice
¼   cup finely chopped scallions
2   tablespoons minced shallots
¼   cup butter

1   cup flour
½   cup half and half
5   ounces Alaskan king crabmeat, cut into small pieces
½   cup dry white wine
white pepper to taste
hot red pepper sauce to taste
½   cup fresh bread crumbs
3   large eggs
1   cup clarified butter

LEMON SAUCE:
2   tablespoons white wine vinegar
2   tablespoons chopped shallots
3 to 4 peppercorns

1   bay leaf
½   cup dry white wine
juice of ½ lemon
½   cup butter, softened
1   cup whipping cream

- Season fish fillets with salt and lemon juice. Marinate in refrigerator 1 hour.
- While fish is marinating, sauté scallions and shallots in ¼ cup butter until tender, using a large skillet.
- Add 2 tablespoons flour to make a creamy roux. Simmer several minutes to cook flour; add half and half.
- After mixture comes to a boil, simmer and add crabmeat, wine and seasonings.
- Remove from heat; stir in bread crumbs and one egg. The filling should be firm, but spreadable.
- Preheat oven to 350°.
- Spread filling on fish and roll up.

continued

- Beat 2 eggs lightly in bowl.
- Coat rolls first in egg, then in remaining flour.
- Brown in clarified butter, turning only once.
- Remove rolls to buttered pan.
- Bake for 20 to 25 minutes.
- Let rolls set 15 minutes before serving.
- Meanwhile make Lemon Sauce:
  Combine vinegar, shallots, peppercorns and bay leaf in pan; reduce over moderate heat until almost dry, 2 to 3 minutes.
- Add wine, lemon juice and butter.
- Stir in cream.
- Reduce to 1½ cups, about 10 minutes.
- Spoon Lemon Sauce over fish. Serve hot.

Grilled Swordfish

Planning:
Marinate 30 minutes

Preparation Time:
10 minutes

Cooking Time:
Approximately 15 minutes

Yield:
2 to 3 servings

Will become one of your summer favorites

1	pound swordfish fillets	1	tablespoon chopped fresh parsley
2	tablespoons soy sauce		
2	tablespoons fresh orange juice	2	small garlic cloves, finely chopped
1	tablespoon oil	½	teaspoon fresh lemon juice
1	tablespoon catsup		

- Arrange swordfish in single layer in a baking pan.
- Combine all remaining ingredients in small bowl.
- Pour over swordfish and let stand at room temperature for 30 minutes.
- Preheat broiler or heat grill.
- Broil or grill fish for approximately 8 minutes on first side. Turn over and continue cooking until fish flakes easily with fork.

Note: Pierce holes in fish before marinating to let juice soak in. Double recipe if you like extra sauce.

Swordfish Kebobs

A different way to serve seafood

Planning:
Marinate 1 to 2 hours
Need skewers
Mesquite chips for barbecue
(soaked in water 30 minutes)

Preparation Time:
10 minutes

Cooking Time:
10 minutes

Yield:
½ pound per person

Swordfish, cut into kebobs
whole bay leaves

crushed garlic, to taste
bottled Italian dressing

- Cover swordfish, bay leaves and garlic with salad dressing. Marinate 1 to 2 hours.
- Heat grill or broiler.
- Place swordfish on skewers. Cook over hot grill or under broiler approximately 10 minutes, turning frequently.
- Serve at once.

Note: Can also alternate vegetables with swordfish on skewers (tomatoes, small onions, parboiled peppers).

Halibut Baked in Sherry

Planning:
Prepare just before baking

Preparation Time:
5 minutes

Cooking Time:
30 minutes

Yield:
2 to 3 servings

*Simple, fast and elegant.
Perfect for busy days when
company is expected.*

1½ pounds fresh halibut steak
2   tablespoons oil
½   teaspoon salt
1   tablespoon lemon juice

¼   cup dry sherry
1½ teaspoons chopped fresh parsley

- Preheat oven to 350°.
- Brush the bottom of baking dish with a bit of the oil.
- Place halibut in dish and sprinkle with salt.
- Combine remaining oil, lemon juice, sherry and parsley. Brush some of this mixture on fish.
- Bake uncovered about 30 minutes or until fish flakes. Baste fish 2 or 3 times while baking.

Broiled Tarragon Fish

Preparation Time:
5 minutes

Cooking Time:
10 minutes

Yield:
Sauce covers 2 fillets

Basic but appealing

¼   cup vegetable or safflower oil
1   tablespoon lemon juice
½   teaspoon tarragon

½   teaspoon salt
⅛   teaspoon pepper
¼   cup white wine (optional)
white fish — sole or flounder

- Preheat broiler.
- Combine oil, lemon juice, tarragon, salt, pepper and optional white wine until well blended.
- Place fish in glass broiling dish and cover with sauce.
- Broil on middle rack of oven about 10 minutes.

Herb Fish in Foil

Preparation Time:
10 minutes

Cooking Time:
30 minutes

Yield:
4 to 6 servings

The recipe for cooks nervous about preparing fish. The foil keeps fish odors under control.

2 **pounds fish (flounder, sole, cod or haddock)**
3 **medium onions, sliced thin**
3 **medium tomatoes, chopped small**
1 **teaspoon salt**
½ **teaspoon pepper**
pinch of thyme, tarragon and parsley (fresh or dried)
4 **tablespoons margarine or butter**

- Preheat oven to 400°.
- Place fish on heavy duty foil. Top with onion slices.
- Continue to layer fish pieces with tomatoes, salt, pepper, herbs and butter.
- Wrap foil tightly, making sure edges are secure.
- Bake for 30 minutes.

Note: May add 2 or 3 teaspoons lemon juice and/or 1 or 2 minced garlic cloves.

Cleanup is a cinch!

Panfried Flounder with Lemon-Basil Tartar Sauce

Planning:
Sauce and seasoning may be made ahead

Preparation Time:
20 minutes

Cooking Time:
10 to 15 minutes

Yield:
4 servings

Add fresh fish to this make-ahead seasoned sauce to have the perfect combination for the busy but fussy cook.

1 egg
¼ cup milk
1 cup flour

2 pounds flounder fillets, cleaned and wiped dry
oil for frying

SEASONING MIX:
1 tablespoon salt
1 teaspoon onion powder
1 teaspoon paprika
⅛ teaspoon cayenne pepper
½ teaspoon garlic powder

¼ teaspoon black pepper
¼ teaspoon dry mustard
½ teaspoon dried oregano
½ teaspoon dried thyme

TARTAR SAUCE:
½ cup mayonnaise
1½ teaspoons lemon juice

½ teaspoon dried basil
dash hot pepper sauce

- Combine egg and milk in bowl.
- Thoroughly combine seasoning mix in small bowl and add 1½ tablespoons mix to 1 cup of flour.
- Rub remaining seasoning mix into fish.
- Heat oil (about ¼-inch high) in large skillet until hot.
- Dip each fillet into egg, then into flour mixture and fry until nicely browned on both sides.
- Drain on paper towels.
- Serve warm with lemon-basil tartar sauce.

TARTAR SAUCE:
- Combine all ingredients until well blended.

Catch-of-the-Day Bouillabaisse

Preparation Time:
30 minutes

Cooking Time:
20 to 30 minutes

Yield:
4 servings

A bouillabaisse at its best with a marvelous fragrance

2 to 3 pounds fish fillets (pollock, scrod, haddock or any firm white fish)
2 tablespoons olive oil
2 tablespoons butter
2 tablespoons minced fresh parsley
3 medium onions, sliced
1 tablespoon minced fresh basil (or 1 teaspoon dried)
¼ teaspoon saffron
2 bay leaves
pinch crushed red pepper
2 cloves garlic, pressed
2 cups coarsely chopped Italian plum tomatoes
1 cup tomato purée
½ cup dry white wine
salt and pepper to taste
½ cup Greek olives, pitted and cut in half

- Cut fish into chunks and set aside.
- In a large skillet or pot, heat oil and butter.
- Sauté parsley, onions, herbs and crushed red pepper over medium heat until onions are wilted.
- Add garlic and sauté a bit longer.
- Add tomatoes, tomato purée, wine and salt and pepper. Simmer to blend flavors.
- Add fish chunks and olives. Raise heat to medium and cook until fish is cooked through. Taste for seasoning.

Note: Serve with French bread and a salad.

If fresh clams or mussels are available a few may be added. Be sure they are well scrubbed.

Could be served over angel hair pasta.

Serve in warmed bowls.

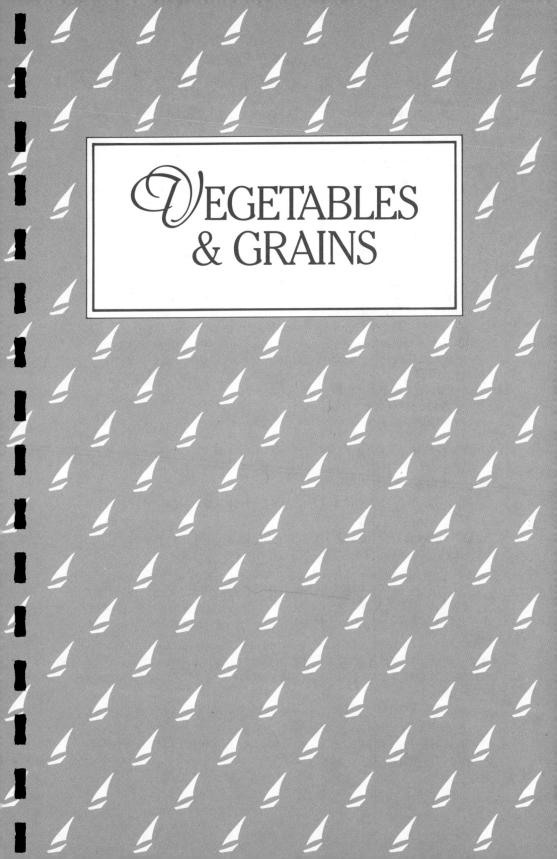

VEGETABLES
& GRAINS

Vegetable Packages

A make-ahead vegetable with impressive presentation

Planning:
May be made ahead

Preparation Time:
15 minutes

Cooking Time:
A few minutes per vegetable for initial parboiling

Reheating Time:
5 minutes

Yield:
Variable

Vegetables of your choice (Choose 3 to 4 seasonal vegetables. Be conscious of colors, i.e., asparagus, carrots and yellow squash are pretty)
Green scallion tops — One long green top for each desired serving

butter (about ½ tablespoon per serving)
salt and pepper to taste
parsley or other desired herb for garnish

- Cut vegetables (such as carrots, zucchini, turnips) into logs of even length (about 3-inches x ¼-inch). Vegetables such as green beans or asparagus leave whole.

- Blanch vegetables separately until just tender. Drain, cool and set aside.

- Make "ribbons" for bundles by blanching the longest green scallion tops for 5 seconds. Drain.

- Group a few logs of each selected vegetables. Place on top of a scallion "ribbon." Tie veggies up with the scallion "ribbon." Make one bundle of vegetables per person. The scallion "ribbons" can be tied in bows or just knots with the extra ribbon trimmed off.

- When ready to serve, braise bundles in butter in a covered skillet over a flow flame. Cook until just heated through. Season with salt and pepper and garnish with parsley or any other appropriate herb.

- To reheat in a microwave, arrange bundles in a starburst pattern in a round microwave-safe dish. Brush with melted butter and cover with vented plastic wrap. Heat at medium high for a few minutes or just until heated through.

Preparation Time:
20 minutes

Cooking Time:
30 minutes

Yield:
8 servings

Summer Vegetables Provencal

A wholesome and colorful way to enjoy a variety of fresh produce.

¼ cup corn oil
1 medium eggplant, peeled, halved and sliced
3 medium zucchini, scrubbed and sliced
1 cup sliced mushrooms
½ cup green pepper strips
½ cup sliced scallions

2 medium garlic cloves, minced
1 cup cherry tomatoes, halved
½ teaspoon salt
¼ teaspoon pepper
2 cups shredded jarlsberg cheese

- Preheat oven to 350°.
- Heat oil in large skillet and sauté eggplant, browning lightly on both sides; set aside.
- Sauté zucchini, mushrooms, green peppers, scallions and garlic several minutes.
- Add tomatoes, salt and pepper. Alternate layers of vegetables and cheese in a buttered shallow 1½-quart casserole dish. Sprinkle cheese over all.
- Bake for 30 minutes.

Summer's Essence Green Beans

Colorful and tasty, this recipe is a wonderful place to use fresh basil.

Planning:
Best if served immediately

Preparation Time:
15 minutes

Cooking Time:
15 minutes

Yield:
4 to 6 servings

1 **pound very ripe fresh tomatoes OR 1 cup canned Italian peeled plum tomatoes, cut up with their juice**
1½ **pounds fresh green beans**
⅓ **cup extra virgin olive oil**

2 **teaspoons garlic, coarsely chopped**
salt
black pepper
1 **cup fresh basil leaves, chopped**

- To peel fresh tomatoes, put them in a pot of boiling water. Return the water to the boil, scald for 30 seconds, drain and cool. Peel the tomatoes when cool enough to handle.
- Cut the tomatoes into large pieces.
- Snap off ends of green beans and rinse green beans in cold water.
- Using a skillet large enough to hold all the green beans, sauté the garlic in the olive oil over medium heat. Cook until garlic turns golden.
- Add tomatoes and cook for about 5 to 6 minutes.
- Add green beans, turn down heat to medium. Add salt and pepper to taste. Cook stirring occasionally until the beans are tender yet firm.
- If the juices in the pan are too watery, remove beans with a slotted spoon, turn up heat and boil away excess liquid.
- Return beans to the pan, mix in basil leaves and serve.

Garlicky Green Bean Bundles

Planning:
May be assembled in advance

Preparation Time:
15 minutes

Cooking Time:
10 minutes

Yield:
8 servings

These beans are as delicious as they are convenient. Try them with a meal of roasted meat. Bake the beans just when you have removed the roast and are slicing it.

1	**pound fresh green beans**	8	**cloves garlic, crushed**
4	**tablespoons butter**	8	**slices bacon**

- Preheat oven to 350°.
- Cook beans briefly in water (or they may be steamed) until just cooked but still crispy. Drain.
- Melt butter and stir in the crushed garlic.
- Cook bacon for a few minutes until it is slightly cooked but still limp and workable.
- Divide beans into individual bundles and wrap each with a bacon slice. Place in a baking dish in a single layer.
- Drizzle with the garlic butter.
- Bake for 10 minutes.

Grilled Eggplant and Tomato

Serve right from the foil for a different barbecue side dish.

Planning:
Requires a barbecue

Preparation Time:
5 minutes

Cooking Time:
30 minutes

Yield:
8 servings

4   **tablespoons olive oil**
½   **cup chopped fresh basil**
¼   **cup chopped fresh oregano**
3   **garlic cloves, minced**
fresh ground pepper
2   **large eggplants**

1   **pound tomatoes, cored and cut in thin slices**
2   **tablespoons olive oil**
2   **tablespoons chopped fresh basil**

- Preheat grill to medium.
- Mix olive oil, basil, oregano, garlic and pepper in a bowl.
- Cut each eggplant vertically into 6 to 8 slices — starting from the bottom and leaving top intact. Place each eggplant in double thickness of foil large enough to wrap.
- Brush each slice of eggplant with oil mixture and insert tomato slices between slices of eggplant. Spread eggplant to look like a fan.
- Wrap tightly with foil and place on grill rack. Cook with the grill cover closed about 30 minutes.
- Unwrap eggplant and drizzle remaining oil and basil over all.
- Serve in foil.

Cherry Tomatoes Provencal

Preparation Time:
10 minutes

Cooking Time:
12 minutes

Yield:
8 servings

Well-seasoned and simple

2 cups cherry tomatoes, halved
4 tablespoons finely chopped scallions
4 tablespoons chopped parsley
1 teaspoon dried basil
½ teaspoon chopped garlic
½ cup dry seasoned bread crumbs
½ teaspoon salt
pepper to taste
3 to 4 tablespoons olive oil

- Preheat oven to 400°.
- Place tomatoes in a single layer in an oiled baking dish.
- In a small bowl, toss together the scallions, 2 tablespoons parsley, basil, garlic, bread crumbs, salt and pepper.
- Spread over the tomatoes. Drizzle oil over all.
- Bake for 12 minutes. Garnish with remaining parsley.

Italian Swiss Chard

Planning:
Prepare at serving time

Preparation Time:
5 minutes

Cooking Time:
6 minutes

Yield:
4 servings

If you aren't familiar with Swiss chard, let this simple recipe be your introduction.

1 **bunch Swiss chard**
2 **garlic cloves, sliced**
3 **tablespoons olive oil**

½ **6-ounce can tomato paste**
   salt to taste

- Wash Swiss chard. Slice into 1-inch strips.
- In a medium saucepan, sauté sliced garlic in olive oil for 1 minute.
- Add washed Swiss chard and tomato paste. Cover saucepan and steam over medium-low heat until Swiss chard is tender (about 4 to 5 minutes).
- Taste and add salt if necessary. Serve immediately, using a slotted spoon to remove Swiss chard from the saucepan.

Incredible Brussel Sprouts

Planning:
Best if made right before serving

Preparation Time:
5 minutes

Cooking Time:
20 minutes

Yield:
4 servings

These have a nice nutty, garlicky flavor. If you aren't already a devotee of brussel sprouts, this recipe might change your mind.

2 **cups brussel sprouts**
2 **tablespoons olive oil**

2 **garlic cloves, crushed**
   salt and pepper to taste

- Trim brussel sprouts and cut in half.
- In a skillet, warm olive oil and sauté the crushed garlic just until it starts to turn golden.
- Add the brussel sprouts to the skillet and cook over a medium-low flame, turning occasionally until they become light brown and tender, about 15 to 20 minutes. Add salt and pepper to taste and serve immediately.

Planning:
May be prepared a few hours
in advance

Preparation Time:
5 minutes

Cooking Time:
45 minutes

Yield:
6 servings

Oven-Roasted Rosemary Potatoes

Super simple with superb results

5 medium red potatoes (about 2 pounds), unpeeled	salt and pepper to taste
3 to 4 tablespoons unsalted butter	fresh rosemary, chopped (dry may be substituted)

- Preheat oven to 425°.
- Wash potatoes and cut into ¼-inch slices.
- Melt butter in a small saucepan. Pour half the butter into a 9x13-inch baking dish.
- Layer potato slices in rows, overlapping them. Sprinkle with salt, pepper and rosemary to taste. Drizzle remaining butter over all and cover baking dish with aluminum foil.
- Bake for 20 minutes. Remove the foil cover carefully and continue baking for an additional 25 minutes or until potatoes are nicely browned and tender.

Elegant Scalloped Potatoes

Easy and versatile

Planning:
May be made ahead

Preparation Time:
15 minutes

Cooking Time:
25 to 30 minutes

Yield:
6 servings

6	potatoes	¼	cup butter or margarine
2	tablespoons butter or margarine	1½	cups sour cream
⅓	cup chopped onion	1	teaspoon dill weed
2	cups shredded Cheddar cheese	1	teaspoon salt
		¼	teaspoon pepper

- Preheat oven to 450°.
- Boil potatoes in their skins just until tender (about 15 minutes). Cool, peel and cut into thin slices.
- In a large skillet, using 2 tablespoons butter, sauté onion until translucent and limp.
- Add Cheddar cheese and ¼ cup butter to onions in the skillet. Stir until almost melted. Remove from heat and blend in sour cream, dill, salt and pepper.
- Fold in sliced potatoes. Turn into a greased 2-quart casserole. (At this point, the casserole may be refrigerated. Return to room temperature before baking.)
- Bake the casserole for 25 minutes.

Savory Potato-Carrot Sauté

Preparation Time:
20 minutes

Cooking Time:
30 to 40 minutes

Yield:
4 to 6 servings

Herby and spicy

½	cup butter or margarine	¾	teaspoon salt
4	cups unpeeled potatoes, sliced ¼-inch thick	¾	teaspoon garlic powder
		¾	teaspoon dry mustard
2	cups carrots, sliced ½-inch thick	½	teaspoon celery or caraway seed
1	cup onions, sliced ¼-inch thick	⅛	teaspoon pepper

- In a heavy 10-inch skillet, melt butter.
- Add remaining ingredients and cover tightly.
- Cook over medium heat turning with spatula occasionally for 10 to 15 minutes.
- Uncover and continue cooking, turning frequently, until potatoes and carrots are tender and potatoes start to crisp and turn brown (15 to 25 minutes).

Note: If vegetables start to stick, add a few drops of water while cooking.

Carrot Purée with Cognac

A standout sidedish!

Planning:
May be made ahead

Preparation Time:
20 minutes

Cooking Time:
15 minutes

Yield:
4 servings

1½ **pounds carrots (about 10 to 12), peeled and chopped**
¼ **cup butter, melted**
1 **teaspoon salt**
¼ **teaspoon freshly ground pepper**
2 **tablespoons heavy cream**
2 **teaspoons cognac or to taste**

- Cook carrots in water until tender. Drain.

- In a food processor, process ⅓ carrots with metal blade until finely chopped. Repeat 2 times adding remaining carrots each time. If necessary, stop the processor and scrape down.

- Add butter, salt and pepper. Process further for 30 seconds.

- Add cream and cognac and process until combined. Taste and adjust seasoning.

Note: If made ahead, reheat in microwave.

If cognac is not appropriate, substitute chicken broth or additional cream.

Holiday Baked Squash

Planning:
May be prepared in advance

Preparation Time:
30 minutes

Cooking Time:
45 minutes

Yield:
8 servings

Yellow summer squash at its finest. Like the center hall colonial homes which dot our communities, this recipe reflects the New England influence in the Sound Shore area.

3	pounds yellow summer squash	2	eggs
½	cup finely chopped onions	6	tablespoons butter or margarine
⅔	cup crushed saltine crackers (about 20)	1	tablespoon sugar
½	teaspoon pepper	½	teaspoon salt or to taste
			paprika for garnish

- Preheat oven to 375°.
- Wash and cut squash in ¼-inch slices. Steam until tender.
- Drain well (pressing out liquid) and mash.
- Add onions, ½ of cracker crumbs, pepper, eggs, 4 tablespoons of butter, sugar and salt. Pour into shallow 2-quart baking dish.
- Melt remaining 2 tablespoons butter. Drizzle on top and sprinkle with remaining cracker crumbs. Sprinkle paprika on top for color.
- Bake uncovered for 45 minutes. Remove from oven and serve immediately.

Note: Excellent with Thanksgiving turkey, Christmas crown roast of pork or with Easter's leg of lamb.

Honey-Bean Squash

Colorful and tasty, this dish will add to any family meal and impress any honored guest.

Planning:
Best if served just after preparation

Preparation Time:
5 minutes

Cooking Time:
1 hour

Yield:
8 servings

2   **medium acorn squash**
½   **pound fresh green beans, cut on the diagonal OR 1 package frozen cut green beans**

½   **cup sweet butter, divided**
1 to 3 tablespoons honey
¼   **cup pine nuts**
nutmeg, freshly grated

- Preheat oven to 350°.
- Wash the squash and place on a baking sheet. Place on the middle rack of oven and bake for 1 hour or until squash are done. (They will be uniformly soft and may be juicy.)
- Meanwhile, cook green beans until tender crisp. Drain. Add ¼ cup butter, honey and pine nuts. Toss to mix.
- When squash are cooked, remove to a cutting board. Remove the stem with the tip of a knife and then cut in half with a large, sharp knife. Scoop seeds out of each half.
- Place a pat of remaining butter in each half and allow it to melt. Spoon bean-honey mixture into the cavity and dust with a grating of fresh nutmeg.
- Cut each squash piece in half, being sure honey-bean filling is equally divided and balanced in the quartered squash. Serve at once.

Note: This recipe may be easily doubled or halved.

Zucchini Soufflé

Delicious and easy. Even a novice will have great success with this soufflé.

Planning:
May be made ahead

Preparation Time:
10 minutes

Cooking Time:
35 to 45 minutes

Yield:
8 servings

4   large zucchini, shredded
1   large onion, finely chopped
½ cup vegetable oil
1   cup biscuit baking mix
4   eggs, beaten

½ cup Parmesan cheese, grated
1   teaspoon salt
pepper to taste
3   tablespoons dry dill weed

- Preheat oven to 350°.*
- In a large bowl, combine shredded zucchini, chopped onion, and oil.
- Blend in baking mix and eggs.
- Add cheese, salt, pepper and dill. Mix well. Spoon into a 2-quart casserole dish.
- Bake 35 to 45 minutes or until top of soufflé is brown. Serve immediately.

*Recipe may be prepared a few hours in advance of serving. After spooning soufflé into casserole dish, cover and refrigerate. Bring casserole to room temperature, preheat oven and bake when desired.

Zucchini Creole

A great combination of late summer vegetables. The zucchini can retain some crispness in this flavorful dish.

Planning:
May be prepared a few hours in advance

Preparation Time:
15 minutes

Cooking Time:
10 minutes on stovetop
45 to 60 minutes in oven

Yield:
8 servings

6 **medium-sized zucchini, sliced thin**
3 **tablespoons butter**
3 **tablespoons flour**
2 **cups chopped ripe tomatoes***
1 **small green pepper, chopped**
1 **small onion, chopped**

1 **teaspoon salt**
1 **tablespoon brown sugar**
½ **bay leaf**
2 **whole cloves**
   unseasoned bread crumbs
   butter
½ **cup grated Cheddar cheese**

- Preheat oven to 350°.
- Put sliced zucchini in a large casserole dish.
- In a medium saucepan, melt the butter. Add the flour. Heat through while stirring for 2 minutes.
- Add tomatoes, green pepper, onion, salt, brown sugar, bay leaf, and whole cloves. Cook over medium heat for 5 minutes while stirring.
- Pour over zucchini. Cover the top of the casserole with bread crumbs. Dot lightly with butter. Top with a sprinkling of grated cheese.
- Bake for 45 to 60 minutes until zucchini are tender. Serve immediately.

*Drained, canned tomatoes can be substituted.

Spiced Spinach Purée

Planning:
May be made ahead

Preparation Time:
15 minutes

Cooking Time:
6 minutes

Yield:
4 servings

*More flavorful than your mother's
creamed spinach*

1 **pound fresh spinach, well washed and trimmed OR 1 10-ounce package frozen spinach, thawed**	1 **small onion, finely chopped**
1 **cup half and half, divided**	2 **tablespoons flour**
2 **tablespoons butter or margarine**	¼ **teaspoon salt**
	¼ **teaspoon ground allspice**

- In a Dutch oven over high heat, bring fresh spinach and ¼ cup water to a boil. Cover and cook for 1 minute. Expect the volume of spinach to decrease. Drain in a sieve or colander. Press out excess liquid. (If using frozen spinach, don't cook spinach. Just press excess liquid out of thawed spinach in a sieve.)

- Put spinach and ¼ cup half and half into a food processor. Process until smooth and set aside.

- In a 2-quart saucepan, melt butter or margarine. Add onion. Cook until tender. Stir in flour, salt and allspice.

- Add the remaining ¾ cup half and half to the flour and butter mixture. Stir until well-blended. Cook, stirring constantly, until mixture boils and thickens.

- Stir in puréed spinach. If making ahead, it may be set aside at this point.

- At serving time, reheat gently until heated through.

Macadamia Nut Rice

Subtle nut flavor

Preparation Time:
5 minutes

Cooking Time:
30 minutes

Yield:
4 servings

$1\frac{1}{3}$ cups uncooked long grain rice

3 tablespoons unsalted butter

$\frac{1}{2}$ teaspoon crushed dried hot red peppers

$\frac{1}{2}$ cup chopped macadamia nuts

- Drop rice into boiling salted water. Heat to boiling, stirring once. Reduce heat and let simmer until rice is just tender (12 to 15 minutes).

- Drain rice in a colander. Place colander over steaming water. Cover rice with a single sheet of paper towel. Let steam at least 15 minutes.

- In a small skillet, melt butter. Stir in the hot pepper and macadamia nuts. Cook, stirring constantly until nuts begin to turn golden.

- Toss with the hot rice in a bowl. Serve immediately.

grace huntley pugh ©

PLAYLAND

Easily reached by bus, rail or parkway, frequently seen on the silver screen, Playland in Rye is the amusement park for all seasons. From June through September, salt and fresh water swimming, the Dragon Coaster, kiddyland, cotton candy and Colonel Custard beckon. It's a winter playland, too, with the ice rink and casino where local high school hockey teams, figure skating clubs and the New York Rangers work out.

When Playland opened in the 1920's, it was the wonder of the Atlantic Coast and it remains one of its jewels unique in its art deco charm and landscaped grounds. On a summer's night, seen from across Playland Lake, with its twinkling lights, fairy spires and the gurgle of the caliope, Playland is Oz.

Spiced Lemon Rice

A tart but not strong rice dish. Its yellow color adds a nice touch on a dinner plate.

Planning:
Better if prepared just before serving time

Preparation Time:
5 minutes

Cooking Time:
Rice — 20 minutes
Spice — 5 minutes

Yield:
6 servings

2 **cups water**
1 **cup rice**
4 **tablespoons sweet butter**
1 **teaspoon salt**

2 **teaspoons ground turmeric**
1 **teaspoon ground mustard**
3 **tablespoons fresh lemon juice**

- In a large saucepan, bring 2 cups water to a boil. Slowly add rice and return to a boil. Cover and simmer without stirring for 20 minutes or just until the liquid is absorbed.
- Ten minutes before rice is finished cooking, melt the butter in a skillet. Add salt, turmeric and mustard and cook over medium heat for 5 minutes to blend flavors.
- Pour the seasoned butter over the cooked rice. Add lemon juice and stir well to blend in spices and juice.
- Serve immediately.

Wild Rice Pilaf

Prepare this recipe mix and always have on hand a wonderful side dish that will complement many poultry, game or beef meals.

Planning:
This is made ahead. Store and cook as needed.

Preparation Time:
20 minutes

Baking Time:
10 to 15 minutes

Cooking Time:
50 minutes on stovetop for final preparation

Yield:
60 servings

3   **cups wild rice**
2   **cups dry lentils**
2   **cups raisins**
1½ **cups dried chopped mushrooms**
1   **cup barley**
½   **cup shelled sunflower seeds**
3   **tablespoons instant powdered beef bouillon**

3   **tablespoons dried parsley flakes**
2   **tablespoons dried onion flakes**
1   **tablespoon dried basil**
2   **teaspoons garlic powder**
½   **teaspoon cinnamon**
½   **teaspoon pepper**

- Preheat oven to 300°.
- Rinse rice and lentils. Drain. Spread on a baking sheet and heat in oven for 10 to 15 minutes or until dry. Stir frequently during the baking process.
- Cool the rice and lentils.
- While the rice is baking and cooling, combine all the remaining ingredients in a large bowl. Finally, stir in the cooled rice and lentils.
- Store in an airtight container.

TO MAKE 2 SERVINGS:

- Combine ⅓ cup pilaf mix with 1 cup water. Bring to a boil, reduce heat, cover and simmer for 50 minutes.
- If desired, add chopped carrots, broccoli or other vegetables midway through the cooking time.

Note: This is a great gift: Put in a pretty jar with a tag that includes the instructions for preparing two servings.

Barley Pilaf

*Excellent substitute for
rice dishes*

Planning:
May be made a few hours
ahead

Preparation Time:
15 minutes

Cooking Time:
40 minutes

Yield:
8 to 10 servings

6   tablespoons butter
1½ cups chopped leeks, white
    part only
1¼ cups thinly sliced celery
2   cups pearl barley
3   bay leaves

1   teaspoon dried thyme
freshly ground pepper
3½ cups beef stock
½   cup red wine
½   cup fresh minced parsley
¼   cup snipped fresh chives

- Preheat oven to 350°.

- Melt butter in a heavy ovenproof casserole over medium-low heat. Add leeks and celery and cook until soft, stirring occasionally, about 6 minutes.

- Add barley. Cook and stir for 3 minutes.

- Add bay leaves, thyme and a generous amount of pepper. Mix in stock and wine. Bring to a boil. Remove from stove.

- Cover tightly and bake until liquid is absorbed, about 35 to 40 minutes.

- Remove from oven. Stir in parsley and chives. Serve immediately.

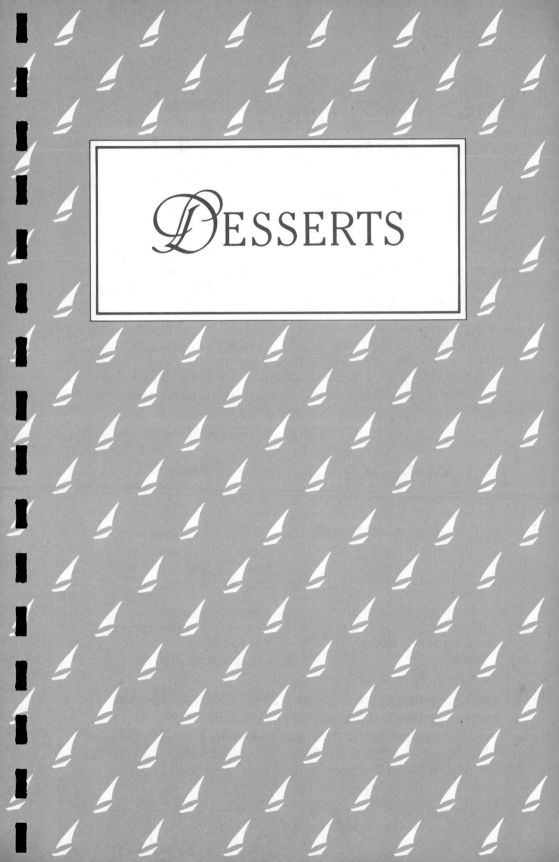

DESSERTS

Raspberry Zinfandel Sauce

Planning:
Can be made ahead

Preparation Time:
5 minutes

Cooking Time:
20 minutes

Yield:
1½ cups

A recipe to appreciate how wonderful food is when using real vanilla bean flavor.

3   **cups red zinfandel wine**
1½ **cups frozen unsweetened raspberries**
¾   **cup sugar**

1   **6-inch and 1   3-inch piece vanilla bean, split lengthwise**

- In a medium saucepan, combine zinfandel, frozen berries, sugar and vanilla beans. Bring to a boil, reduce heat and simmer 5 minutes. Increase heat and boil until reduced to 1½ cups, stirring occasionally. This will take approximately 15 minutes.
- Strain berry mixture through a sieve, pressing berries to extract as much pulp as possible. Cool to room temperature.

Note: Garnish with almonds, mint or fresh raspberries.

Hot Fudge Sauce

Planning:
Can be made ahead

Preparation Time:
10 minutes

Cooking Time:
5 to 10 minutes

Yield:
12 servings

This is wonderful on any ice cream, cake roll, or even just on a spoon!

8   **ounces sweet German chocolate**
¼   **cup butter (½ stick)**
1   **cup of sugar**
1   **pinch of salt**

1   **cup heavy cream**
3   **teaspoons coffee liqueur (or to taste)**
1   **teaspoon vanilla**

- Over moderate heat in a double boiler, melt chocolate, stirring constantly. Don't let it boil.
- Add butter, sugar, salt and cream. Cook and stir for a few minutes until thickened. Remove from heat. Add coffee liqueur and vanilla.

Note: Will keep for 2 weeks in the refrigerator. Reheat gently.

Chocolate Lover's Cake
(A Chocolate Sheet Cake)

Preparation Time:
20 minutes

Cooking Time:
20 minutes

Yield:
20 servings

This quick cake will serve a crowd of chocolate lovers.

CAKE:

1 cup butter	2 cups flour
1 cup water	1 teaspoon baking soda
¼ cup cocoa	½ cup sour cream
2 cups sugar	2 eggs, beaten

ICING:

½ cup margarine (not butter)	1 pound confectioners' sugar
6 tablespoons milk	1 cup chopped walnuts or
¼ cup cocoa	pecans (optional)
1 teaspoon vanilla	

- Preheat oven to 375°.
- In a saucepan measuring 6 to 8 inches across top, put butter, water and cocoa. Bring to a boil.
- Measure sugar, flour and baking soda into a mixing bowl and stir a little.
- When the mixture in saucepan boils, pour immediately into dry ingredients. (Don't wash saucepan yet!)
- Beat batter well for about 30 seconds. Stir in sour cream and beat in eggs.
- Pour into well-buttered 16x11-inch jelly roll pan; spread smooth.
- Bake for 20 minutes.
- While cake is baking, prepare ICING: In same saucepan as used above, melt together margarine, milk and cocoa. When it comes to a boil, add vanilla.
- Transfer Icing mixture to a small bowl of electric mixer and pour in confectioners' sugar while beating. When all the sugar has been incorporated, beat for a few seconds at high speed. Stir in the nuts, if desired.
- As soon as the cake is removed from the oven, spread on icing with a rubber spatula. Cool.

Bee-Sting Cake

This cake is beautiful with a professional appearance even though it is not difficult to make.

Planning:
May be made ahead

Preparation Time:
25 minutes

Cooking Time:
25 minutes

Yield:
8 to 10 servings

CAKE:

½ cup butter
1 cup finely ground
  unblanched almonds
½ cup sugar
2 tablespoons milk
2 teaspoons vanilla
½ cup butter
⅓ cup sugar

1 egg
2 cups sifted flour
2 teaspoons baking powder
½ teaspoon salt
2 tablespoons milk
confectioners' sugar (for top of cake)

BUTTER CREAM FILLING:

¼ cup sweet butter, softened
1 egg yolk
1 cup confectioners' sugar

1 teaspoon vanilla
heavy cream (to thin filling if it is too stiff)

RASPBERRY FILLING:

1 cup raspberry jam
  (preferably seedless)

CAKE:

- Preheat oven to 400°.

- In a saucepan, melt ½ cup butter. Blend in the ground unblanched almonds, ½ cup sugar, milk and vanilla. Bring to a boil. Remove from heat and cool.

- Cream ½ cup butter with ⅓ cup sugar until it is smooth. Slowly beat in egg.

- Sift the flour with the baking powder and salt.

- Add the dry ingredients to the butter mixture alternately with the 2 tablespoons milk.

- Spoon the batter into a well-buttered 8-inch springform pan. Pour almond mixture over the batter and spread evenly. Bake for 25 minutes. Cool.

continued

- Prepare Raspberry Filling and Butter Cream Filling as directed below while the cake is baking and cooling.
- After the cake has cooled, remove the cake from the pan and slice in half horizontally.
- On the bottom layer of cake, spread all of the Butter Cream Filling. Carefully spread all of the Raspberry Filling over the Butter Cream.
- Reassemble the cake by replacing the top layer of cake over the fillings. Sprinkle the top of the cake with sifted confectioners' sugar.

BUTTER CREAM FILLING:

- Cream the butter until soft in a small bowl with an electric mixer. Add the egg yolk.
- Beat in the confectioners' sugar, 2 tablespoons at a time, and beat until blended and fluffy. Beat in the vanilla. If the Butter Cream is too thick, add a little heavy cream.

RASPBERRY FILLING:

- Heat the raspberry jam. If the jam has seeds, put it through a fine sieve to remove most of the seeds. Let jam cool slightly.

Note: When slicing the cake in half horizontally, use a long serrated knife and the bottom of the springform pan. To remove the top layer easily without breaking it, slide the bottom of the pan between the two layers as you cut the cake.

Norwegian Gold Cake

---

*This is a delicious, very moist one-bowl cake. It may be served with just a decorative sprinkle of powdered sugar. This lovely cake is also delicious served with **Raspberry Zinfandel Sauce** or **Hot Fudge Sauce**. Left over Norwegian Gold Cake may be used for **Lemon Mousse Trifle.***

Planning:
A standing electric mixer is very helpful because of the lengthy beating time for this cake (at least 10 minutes).

Preparation Time:
20 minutes

Cooking Time:
1 hour

Yield:
14 servings

1⅓ cups sifted flour
1 cup butter, softened
5 eggs
1½ cups sugar

1½ teaspoons baking powder
1 teaspoon vanilla
1 teaspoon grated lemon rind (optional)

- Preheat the oven to 325°.
- Mix flour and butter in a mixing bowl using an electric mixer on low speed until blended.
- Add the eggs, one at a time, beating well after each egg.
- Slowly add sugar to the mixture. Beat well.
- Beat in baking powder.
- Add vanilla and optional lemon rind. Beat well.
- Pour batter into greased and floured 10-inch Bundt pan and bake for one hour.
- Cool in pan for 10 minutes before removing from pan.

Apple Pound Cake

Sweet goodness soaked with sauce

Planning:
Tastes better when prepared the day before

Preparation Time:
30 minutes

Cooking Time:
1 hour, 20 minutes

Yield:
12 servings

CAKE:
1½ cups vegetable oil
2 cups sugar
3 eggs
3 cups sifted flour
1 teaspoon salt
1 teaspoon baking soda

1½ teaspoons cinnamon
2 teaspoons vanilla
3 large apples, peeled and chopped
1 cup chopped nuts

SAUCE:
½ cup butter
½ cup packed light brown sugar

2 tablespoons milk

- Preheat oven to 350°.
- Combine oil, sugar and eggs in a large mixing bowl. Beat for 3 minutes at medium speed.
- Blend in flour, salt, baking soda, cinnamon and vanilla.
- Fold in apples and chopped nuts.
- Bake in a well-greased and floured tube pan for 1 hour and 20 minutes. (Test for doneness at 1 hour with a toothpick.)
- Prepare SAUCE: bring sauce ingredients to a boil in a medium saucepan. Cook for 2 minutes.
- Pour sauce on cake while both cake and sauce are hot. Sauce will be thin and soak in.

Coach's Carrot Cake

This cake is moist and delicious. Luckily it has a few healthy touches in its ingredients.

Planning:
If made in advance, cake may be frozen or refrigerated

Preparation Time:
45 minutes

Cooking Time:
30 to 40 minutes

Yield:
12 servings

2 cups whole wheat flour
2 teaspoons baking powder
1½ teaspoons baking soda
1 teaspoon salt
2 teaspoons cinnamon
1 teaspoon nutmeg
2 cups sugar

1½ cups vegetable oil
4 large eggs
2 cups grated, raw carrots
1 13-ounce can crushed, drained pineapple
½ cup chopped pecans

CREAM CHEESE FROSTING:
½ cup butter or margarine, softened
1 8-ounce package cream cheese, softened

1 teaspoon vanilla
1 pound box sifted confectioners' sugar

- Preheat oven to 350°.
- Sift together flour, baking powder, baking soda, salt, cinnamon and nutmeg into a large bowl.
- Add the sugar, oil, and eggs to the flour mixture and mix well.
- Stir the carrots, pineapple and nuts into the batter.
- Pour the batter into an ungreased 13x9x2-inch pan.
- Bake for 30 to 40 minutes.
- While the cake is cooling, prepare the CREAM CHEESE FROSTING: combine butter, cream cheese and vanilla. Beat well. Add confectioners' sugar gradually. Beat vigorously.
- Frost the cake when it is completely cool with the Cream Cheese Frosting.

Fresh Blueberry Batter Cake

*This cake is sweet and simple —
just like summertime vacations at
the beach.*

Planning:
May be made ahead, but
tastes best when warm

Preparation Time:
15 minutes

Cooking Time:
1 hour

Yield:
12 servings

2 cups fresh blueberries
juice of ½ lemon
¾ cup sugar
3 tablespoons butter, softened

1 cup flour, sifted
1 tablespoon baking powder
⅛ teaspoon salt
½ cup milk
1 cup boiling water

TOPPING:
½ teaspoon salt
1 cup sugar

1 tablespoon cornstarch

- Preheat oven to 375°.
- Line a well-greased 8x8x2-inch pan with blueberries. Sprinkle with lemon juice.
- In a large bowl, cream the sugar and butter with an electric mixer.
- In a small bowl, combine the sifted flour, baking powder and salt.
- To the creamed sugar and butter add milk alternately with flour mixture. Pour the batter over the blueberries.
- Prepare TOPPING: combine Topping ingredients in a small bowl and sprinkle over top of the batter. Pour 1 cup of boiling water over all.
- Bake for 1 hour.
- Serve with whipped cream or ice cream.

Five-Spice Gingerbread with Apricot-Pecan Sauce

A well-seasoned gingerbread with a unique sauce

Planning:
Both sauce and cake may be made ahead.

Preparation Time:
15 minutes

Cooking Time:
55 to 60 minutes

Yield:
16 servings

½ teaspoon salt
1½ teaspoons baking soda
1 teaspoon ground ginger
¾ teaspoon ground cinnamon
½ teaspoon ground allspice
½ teaspoon ground nutmeg
½ teaspoon ground cloves
½ cup solid vegetable shortening

1 cup sugar
1 large egg
1 cup pure sugar-cane syrup OR 1 cup molasses OR ½ cup molasses combined with ½ cup light corn syrup
2½ cups sifted all-purpose flour
1 cup hot water

APRICOT PECAN SAUCE:
1½ cups apricot jam
½ cup water
1 teaspoon grated orange peel

½ cup broken pecans

- Preheat oven to 350°.
- Combine the salt, baking soda and spices with the shortening. Mix well in a large bowl with an electric mixer.
- Gradually blend in sugar.
- Beat in egg.
- Add syrup (or molasses or molasses/corn syrup) alternately with flour.
- Add hot water, a little at a time, beating after each addition.
- Turn into a well-greased, well-floured 9x9x2-inch pan.
- Bake for 55 to 60 minutes or until a toothpick inserted in center comes out clean.
- While cake is baking, prepare Apricot Pecan Sauce.

continued

APRICOT PECAN SAUCE:

- Combine the jam, water and orange peel in a small saucepan. Bring to a boil and simmer for 5 minutes, stirring constantly.
- Remove from the heat and stir in the pecans.
- Serve warm over gingerbread.

Almond-Irish Cream Cheesecake

Smooth and Rich

Planning:
Must be made the night before

Preparation Time:
20 minutes

Cooking Time:
7 minutes plus 1½ hours

Yield:
12 servings

CRUST:
- 1½ cups vanilla wafer cookie crumbs
- ½ cup finely chopped almonds, toasted
- ¼ cup butter, melted
- 2 tablespoons sugar
- 1 tablespoon amaretto liqueur

FILLING:
- 3 8-ounce packages cream cheese, softened
- 1 cup sugar
- 4 eggs
- ⅓ cup whipping cream
- ⅓ cup ground blanched almonds
- ¼ cup Irish creme liqueur
- ¼ cup amaretto liqueur

TOPPING:
- 1½ cups sour cream
- 1 tablespoon sugar
- ½ teaspoon vanilla
- ⅓ cup sliced almonds, lightly toasted

CRUST:

- Position rack in center of oven and preheat to 375°.
- Lightly grease bottom and sides of a 9-inch springform pan.
- Mix all crust ingredients in a large bowl until well blended.
- Press mixture into bottom of prepared pan. Bake until edges are brown, about 7 minutes. Cool on rack.
- Reduce oven temperature to 350° for filling.

FILLING:

- Using an electric mixer, beat cream cheese and sugar until light and fluffy.
- Add eggs one at a time, beating well after each addition.
- Add remaining 4 ingredients and beat until well blended.

continued

- Pour filling into prepared crust.
- Bake until edges are light brown and center is almost set (about 1 hour).
- Turn oven off. Cool cake in oven with door open until center is completely set (about 30 minutes).

TOPPING:

- Blend sour cream, sugar and vanilla in a small bowl until smooth.
- Spread over cooled cake. Bake 10 minutes. Cool completely on rack.
- Cover cooled cake with plastic wrap and refrigerate overnight before serving. Garnish with sliced almonds.

Note: Other liqueurs can be substituted (kahlua, creme de cocoa, for example).

Purple Plum Torte

One of the wonderful things to enjoy at the end of the summer.

Planning:
This is best served warm.
Can be frozen and reheated.

Preparation Time:
10 minutes

Cooking Time:
1 hour

Yield:
8 to 10 servings

1   cup sugar
½   cup unsalted butter, softened
1   cup flour
1   teaspoon baking powder
salt to taste
2   eggs
12 purple plums, halved and pitted

1   tablespoon of sugar, more or less depending on the tartness of the fruit
2   teaspoons fresh lemon juice
1   tablespoon cinnamon

- Preheat oven to 350°.
- Cream sugar and butter together until light in color.
- Sift flour with baking powder and salt.
- Mix the eggs and the flour into the sugar-butter mixture.
- Spoon mixture into a 9-inch springform pan. Cover top of batter with plum halves, skin side up. Sprinkle with sugar, lemon juice and cinnamon.
- Bake for 1 hour. Serve warm.

Note: Expect the plums to sink to the bottom of the torte.

Chocolate Torte

Planning:
Make ahead. May be served cold, frozen or at room temperature

Preparation Time:
20 minutes

Cooking Time:
35 minutes

Yield:
8 to 10 servings

What dessert buffet would be complete without one outstanding chocolate dessert? No one will guess how easy it is to make this impressive dessert.

1 **8-ounce bar of semi-sweet chocolate**
8 **ounces unsalted butter, softened**
1 **cup sugar**

8 **eggs, separated**
raspberries or strawberries for garnish
whipped cream for garnish

- Preheat oven to 325°.
- Melt chocolate in a double boiler. Combine butter, sugar and chocolate. Mix well and cool.
- Add egg yolks, two at a time, beating after each addition.
- Whip egg whites until stiff. Fold whites into chocolate mixture.
- Turn ¾ of the batter into a well-greased and floured 9-inch springform pan. Reserve remaining batter for topping.
- Bake for 35 minutes.
- Remove and let stand at room temperature until cool.
- Spread remaining batter on top. Let sit. Batter will remain moist. (Torte may also be frozen or refrigerated if serving at a later time or if a chilled torte is preferred.)
- Remove sides of springform pan when ready to serve.
- Garnish with raspberries or strawberries and whipped cream rosettes.

Note: After greasing your pans for chocolate desserts, try dusting them with cocoa instead of flour.

Chocolate Bread with Vanilla Butter

Planning:
Requires rising time. Prepare Vanilla Butter while bread is rising.

Preparation Time:
4 hours

Cooking Time:
45 to 60 minutes

Yield:
10 to 12 servings

The bread preparation takes a lengthy period (a morning) to complete, but is well worth the effort. The bread is not too sweet, making it excellent to serve with tea or with champagne as part of a cocktail buffet.

1 cup milk	2 eggs, beaten
2 tablespoons butter (not margarine)	3½ cups all-purpose flour
½ cup sugar	⅔ cup sifted Dutch cocoa
1 teaspoon vanilla	butter for greasing bowl
1 package yeast, dissolved in ¼ cup tepid water (about 110°) with 1 tablespoon sugar	coarse sugar

VANILLA BUTTER:

12 tablespoons sweet butter, softened	2 tablespoons vanilla extract
¾ cup confectioners' sugar	

- Scald the milk and remove from the heat. Add the butter, stirring until it melts.
- Add sugar and vanilla. When the mixture is lukewarm (no more than 115°), add the yeast mixture. Add beaten eggs and stir.
- Measure flour and cocoa into a large bowl. Add the yeast mixture and stir. Turn out onto a floured board. While dough is resting, clean and butter a large bowl.
- Knead dough gently for 5 minutes, adding flour as necessary to produce a smooth dough.
- Put dough into the buttered bowl, cover with a damp towel and put in a warm place until the dough doubles in size. This will take one to two hours.
- Prepare VANILLA BUTTER while the dough is rising: cream the butter. Slowly beat in the sugar. Add the vanilla extract. Transfer mixture to a serving bowl, cover and chill.

continued

- Punch down the dough and knead it again 8 to 10 times. Pat into a loaf shape and place in a well-buttered 9x5-inch loaf pan. Cover the dough and let it rise again, but not so much that it doubles (about 45 minutes).

- Preheat oven to 350°. Gently pat top of loaf with coarse sugar and bake one hour on middle rack. After 30 minutes, cover the top of the loaf with foil so it does not burn. Continue baking for another 15 to 30 minutes or until done. (Loaf will sound hollow when tapped with fingers.) Remove loaf from oven and let it cool for 10 minutes in the pan and then turn it out onto a wire rack.

- Slice the Chocolate Bread and serve with Vanilla Butter.

Note: Remove Vanilla Butter from the refrigerator 30 minutes before serving. The butter should be soft and spreadable.

Triple Crown Pecan Pie

This recipe makes 3 wickedly rich pies.

Planning:
Make at least 4 hours in advance to allow pies to set. Pies may be frozen.

Preparation Time:
10 minutes

Cooking Time:
45 minutes

Yield:
3 pies, each serving 8 to 10

$2\frac{1}{4}$ cups sugar
$\frac{3}{4}$ cup brown sugar
3 tablespoons flour
3 cups pecans
3 cups chocolate chips
12 eggs

$1\frac{1}{2}$ cups butter, melted
3 cups white corn syrup
1 tablespoon vanilla
3 tablespoons bourbon (or to taste)
3 unbaked 9-inch pie shells

- Preheat oven to 350°.
- In a very large bowl, combine sugar, brown sugar, flour, pecans and chocolate chips.
- In a separate bowl, beat eggs. Add eggs to dry ingredients and mix well.
- Add melted butter, syrup, vanilla and bourbon. Mix well.
- To ensure that an equal amount of chips and pecans are in each pie shell, ladle the mixture alternately into each shell.
- Bake for 45 minutes. (Center of pie will not set in the baking process, but will become solid when cooled completely.)

Note: Serve with *unsweetened* whipped cream.

Give a pie as a holiday gift.

grace huntley pugh ©

LOUNSBERRY

Standing well back from the hubbub of Rye's Boston Post Road and presenting a serene front to the late twentieth century is Lounsberry. The property rolling down to Long Island Sound was once farmed by a family named Lounsberry. Edward Lamb Parsons liked the name and chose it for the house he built here in 1837. For the next 150 years his descendants would live at Lounsberry. They were lawyers mostly, a congressman and even an anthropologist.

One of the lawyers added the wings to accommodate his law books and growing family. Another planted a mountain magnolia to the right of the house.

The Parsons played croquet on summer afternoons, held dances in the library and entertained at least one president. A framed letter accepting an invitation to tea hung for years in an upstairs bedroom at Lounsberry. The hostess had apparently wondered what her guest would enjoy with his tea. "Madam," President Ulysses S. Grant wrote to Mrs. Parsons, "I would like gingerbread."

253

Lemon Mousse

Enjoy this mousse in its simple form, serve it in a pie shell or present it as a spectacular trifle. **Raspberry Zinfandel Sauce** *is a wonderful addition to all three variations.*

Planning:
Chill at least 2 hours before serving

Preparation Time:
20 minutes

Yield:
8 servings

1½ cups heavy cream
1 envelope unflavored gelatin
¼ cup water
4 egg yolks
⅔ cup sugar

4 egg whites
¼ cup fresh lemon juice
2 tablespoons grated lemon rind
4 paper thin slices of lemon for garnish

PIE:
1 8 or 9-inch baked pie shell

TRIFLE:
slices of pound cake, Norwegian Gold Cake or ladyfingers
Raspberry Zinfandel Sauce (see page 236)

fruit (raspberries, strawberries, bananas, etc.)

MOUSSE:

- Beat cream to stiff consistency and refrigerate.
- Soften gelatin with ¼ cup cold water in a cup. Place cup in a saucepan of boiling water until gelatin becomes a clear liquid. Remove from heat.
- While gelatin is dissolving, beat egg yolks in a large bowl with an electric mixer. Add sugar gradually. Continue mixing until the mixture is thick and lemon-colored, about 5 minutes.
- Beat egg whites until stiff and set aside.
- Add lemon juice, rind and dissolved gelatin to beaten egg yolk mixture using the electric mixer.
- Fold in egg whites by hand. Follow by folding in 2 cups whipped cream.

continued

- Pour mixture into a large glass bowl, dessert glasses or pie shell. Refrigerate at least 2 hours.
- Decorate with remaining whipped cream and lemon slices.

LEMON MOUSSE TRIFLE:
- Line a large glass bowl with slices of cake or ladyfingers.
- Pour ½ cup of Raspberry Zinfandel Sauce over pound cake.
- Top cake slices with any desired fruit.
- Prepare mousse as directed above just through the point of folding in egg whites and whipped cream. Pour mousse on top of cake slices, sauce and fruit.
- Refrigerate for at least two hours.
- Just before serving, garnish with desired fruits, whipped cream and/or lemon slices. Serve with remaining Raspberry Zinfandel Sauce.

An American Fruit Tart

Take advantage of seasonal fruits with this beautiful tart.

Planning:
May be made ahead

Preparation Time:
15 minutes

Cooking Time:
18 to 20 minutes

Yield:
12 servings

CRUST:

1 cup plus 1 tablespoon butter or margarine, softened

½ cup confectioners' sugar
2 cups plus 2 tablespoons flour

FILLING:

11 ounces cream cheese, softened

2 teaspoons vanilla
¾ cup sugar

TOPPING:

6 different fruits from the following: grape halves, strawberry halves, peach slices, pear slices, cherry halves, blueberries, kiwi slices, raspberries, bananas, or apple slices. (Peel apples, bananas, and pears and sprinkle lemon juice over them to prevent browning.)

GLAZE:

3 tablespoons cornstarch
1½ cups orange or pineapple juice

2 teaspoons lemon juice
¾ cup sugar

- Preheat oven to 350°.
- Mix ingredients for crust together in an electric mixer and pat evenly onto a 13½-inch pizza pan. Bake for 18 to 20 minutes. Cool.
- In a clean bowl, mix the filling ingredients with electric mixer and spread onto the cooled crust.
- Arrange the six different fruits in circles on top of filling.
- Make the glaze by boiling all the glaze ingredients in a saucepan over medium heat stirring constantly until thickened.
- Spread glaze over entire tart.
- Cover and refrigerate tart if not eaten immediately.

Note: This recipe may be halved and baked in a 9-inch glass pie pan.

Planning:
Must be made a few hours in advance

Preparation Time:
45 minutes

Cooking Time:
12 minutes

Yield:
6 to 8 servings

White Wine Cream

A light mousse with fresh citrus flavors.

1 cup dry white wine
1 cup sugar
juice of 1 medium orange
   (scant ½ cup)
juice of ½ lemon (about
   3 tablespoons)
1 tablespoon cornstarch

6 egg yolks, room
   temperature
1 cup heavy cream, whipped
additional whipping cream for
   garnish
fresh fruit for garnish

- Combine wine and sugar in a heavy medium saucepan and bring to a boil.
- Combine orange juice, lemon juice and cornstarch in a cup, stirring until smooth.
- Add the juice mixture to wine mixture. Bring to a boil and cook stirring constantly for 1 minute. Remove from the heat.
- Using an electric mixer beat yolks in medium bowl until thick and lemon colored.
- Gradually add about ½ cup hot wine mixture, beating constantly. Then beat yolks back into remaining wine mixture.
- Place over low heat and cook, stirring constantly, until thick (about 8 minutes).
- Transfer custard to a large bowl and let cool completely.
- Fold whipped cream into custard. Divide mixture among parfait glasses. Cover and chill.
- Garnish with additional whipped cream and fresh fruit before serving.

Note: Best if served the day of preparation.

Brandied Apple Cobbler with Vanilla Cream

A little more sophisticated than your grandmother's recipe

Planning:
Vanilla Cream must be prepared at least 4 hours before serving

Preparation Time:
45 minutes

Cooking Time:
1 to 1½ hours

Yield:
14 to 16 servings

VANILLA CREAM:
1 cup heavy cream
½ cup sour cream
1 tablespoon granulated sugar
1 teaspoon vanilla

COBBLER:
2½ pounds firm green apples
¾ cup chopped walnuts
½ cup golden raisins
½ cup currants
½ cup calvados or applejack brandy
2 cups flour
1½ cups sugar
2 teaspoons baking powder
1 cup milk or light cream
½ cup butter, melted
1 teaspoon vanilla
1½ cups packed light brown sugar
2 tablespoons cornstarch
½ teaspoon ground coriander
½ teaspoon salt
¼ teaspoon grated nutmeg
1½ cups apple cider

VANILLA CREAM:

- Blend Vanilla Cream ingredients together in a glass jar and let stand at room temperature until thick (4 hours or overnight). Cover and refrigerate until needed. Will keep 10 days in refrigerator and yield 1½ cups.

COBBLER:

- Preheat oven to 350°.

- Peel, core and thinly slice apples and spread on the bottom of a well-buttered 5-quart baking dish (11x17-inch baking dish or a clean turkey roasting pan). Sprinkle with nuts, raisins, currants and brandy.

continued

- Using a food processor or mixer, blend flour, sugar and baking powder together. Add milk or cream and blend. Add melted butter and vanilla. Mix well. Spoon or pour over apples.
- Blend brown sugar, cornstarch and spices together and sprinkle over cobbler.
- Heat apple cider to a boil and gently spoon over cobbler. Place baking dish on baking sheet and bake in middle of oven for 1 to 1½ hours or until a tester comes out clean.

Note: Calvados or applejack brandy can be purchased at a liquor store.

Planning:
Must be made at least 4 hours in advance

Preparation Time:
40 minutes

Freezing Time:
At least 4 hours

Cooking Time:
10 minutes

Yield:
10 servings

Frozen Chocolate Velvet Cream

This dessert reminds some people of a frozen candy bar.

1½ cups chocolate wafer crumbs
⅓ cup margarine, melted
8 ounces cream cheese, softened
½ cup sugar, divided
1 teaspoon vanilla

2 eggs, separated
6 ounces semi-sweet chocolate chips, melted
1 cup heavy cream, whipped
¾ cup chopped nuts
shaved chocolate and/or whipped cream, for garnish

- Preheat oven to 325°.
- Combine crumbs and margarine. Press into 9-inch springform pan. Bake for 10 minutes.
- Combine softened cream cheese, ¼ cup sugar, and vanilla in a large mixing bowl. Mix with an electric mixer until well blended.
- Blend in 2 beaten egg yolks and melted chocolate.
- Beat egg whites until foamy in a separate bowl. Gradually add ¼ cup sugar, beating to stiff peaks.
- Fold egg whites, whipped cream and nuts into cream cheese mixture. Pour over crust, freeze for at least 4 hours and garnish with shaved chocolate and/or whipped cream.
- To serve, remove sides of springform pan and slice into wedges.

Cranberry Pudding with Eggnog Sauce

A Holiday favorite.

Planning:
May be made ahead

Preparation Time:
20 minutes

Cooking Time:
2 hours

Yield:
10 to 12 servings

6 tablespoons butter, softened	**2½ teaspoons baking powder**
¾ cup sugar	**¼ teaspoon salt**
2 eggs	**½ cup milk**
2¼ cups flour, sifted	**2 cups cranberries**
	½ cup chopped pecans

EGGNOG DESSERT SAUCE:

1 cup butter	**1 cup commercial eggnog**
1¼ cups sugar	**1 tablespoon rum**

- Cream the butter and sugar in a large mixing bowl.
- Add eggs, one at a time, beating well after each addition.
- Sift the flour, baking powder and salt together and add to the creamed mixture alternately with milk. (This will be a very thick mixture.)
- Stir in the cranberries and pecans.
- Turn into a very well greased 6-cup oven-proof bowl or mold. Cover with foil.
- Press foil tightly around edge and secure with string.
- Place mold on a rack in a Dutch oven, saucepan or kettle large enough to hold the mold. Pour enough water into pan to come halfway up mold.
- Bring water to a boil and cover pan tightly. Reduce heat to simmer.
- Steam for 2 hours. Let stand for 10 minutes, then unmold.
- Serve with Eggnog Dessert Sauce.

continued

EGGNOG DESSERT SAUCE:

- Combine the butter, sugar and eggnog in a saucepan. Simmer until heated through, stirring occasionally.
- Stir in rum.

Note: Pudding may be refrigerated for several days or cooked and frozen for several months. Thaw in refrigerator if frozen, then wrap in foil and bake at 325° for 45 minutes to reheat.

Frozen Soufflé Amaretto

With its creamy taste, this is a superlative dessert for a special meal in any season.

Planning:
Prepare the night before.

Preparation Time:
30 minutes

Freezing Time:
At least 10 hours

Yield:
8 to 10 servings

5   egg yolks
3   whole eggs
½   cup superfine sugar
⅓   cup amaretto liqueur
1   cup finely crushed almond macaroon or Italian amaretto cookies

2   cups heavy cream, whipped

- Prepare a 5-cup soufflé or other straight-sided dish by forming a foil collar 2 inches higher than the rim of the dish. Fasten foil with tape or by tying a string just under the rim of the dish. Place bowl in freezer.
- Combine egg yolks, eggs and sugar in a large bowl. Beat with electric mixer at high speed until very thick and light. (This takes 10 to 12 minutes.)
- Turn mixer to low speed. Add the liqueur and crushed cookies.
- Fold in whipped cream with a rubber scraper until no streaks of white remain.
- Pour into prepared dish. Freeze at least 10 hours.
- Remove collar gently from soufflé.
- Roll edge in additional cookie crumbs, if you wish.
- Serve immediately.

Note: No superfine sugar? Processing regular sugar in the food processor or blender for a few seconds will result in superfine sugar. Measure the sugar *after* processing.

grace huntley pugh ©

BUSH HOMESTEAD

Half a century before the Declaration of Independence, Justus Bush, a New York City merchant, purchased a 220 acre farm stretching from King Street down to the Byram River. His son married a local girl, Ruth Lyon, whose family was among the first settlers to this part of Westchester County.

Ruth and Abraham cultivated the land, raised a family and threw in their lot with the patriots during the winter of 1777-1778 when General Israel Putnam made the homestead his headquarters. Their descendants would remain in the homestead on King Street for nearly 200 years.

In the 1920's the Bush family sold the homestead and it became a part of Port Chester's Lyon Park.

Cherry Apple Strudel

This impressive dessert could go anywhere: an elegant afternoon tea or a casual tailgate picnic. Strudels take a bit of effort, but this recipe is worth it! The unique combination of fruits and flaky pastry rivals anything we have tasted in our city's restaurants or countryside inns.

Planning:
May be made in advance

Preparation Time:
30 minutes

Cooking Time:
35 minutes

Yield:
12 to 14 servings

¾	cup hot water	½	teaspoon cinnamon
½	cup raisins	¾	cup unsalted butter, melted
½	package phyllo pastry	3	medium apples, peeled, cored and grated
½	cup packaged unseasoned bread crumbs	1	12-ounce jar cherry preserves
½	cup sugar	1	cup confectioners' sugar
1	cup finely ground walnuts		

- Pour hot water over raisins in a bowl and let stand 5 minutes to plump. Drain and dry.
- Thaw ½ package of phyllo pastry. Unfold carefully. Divide leaves in half (i.e. ¼ package is worked with at a time). Cover remaining phyllo leaves with a damp paper towel to prevent drying.
- Preheat oven to 350°.
- Combine bread crumbs, sugar, nuts and cinnamon in a bowl.
- Brush each leaf of one group of pastry sheets with melted butter. Sprinkle some of the bread crumb mixture evenly over each sheet while stacking. Form a stack of phyllo dough with the butter and bread crumbs between each sheet in the stack.
- Place apples in a colander or sieve. Press firmly against sides with a rubber spatula to expel excess moisture.
- Spread half of the apples and half of the raisins over the lower lengthwise third of phyllo dough.
- Heat preserves over medium heat in a saucepan just until melted and form a liquid. Drain thoroughly. Spread half of the preserves down center of raisins and apples.
- Starting at the lengthwise side with apple-cherry filling, lift and roll pastry (jelly roll fashion).

continued

- Repeat with remaining pastry (¼ of phyllo pastry package).
- Place strudels in a well-buttered jelly roll pan. Brush tops with melted butter.
- Bake for 35 minutes or until golden brown.
- Sprinkle with confectioners' sugar.

Pavlova with Raspberry Sauce

Pavlova is a favorite dessert from Australia invented to honor the famous ballerina. It is meringue-like in appearance with a marsh-mallowy texture inside. The fruits and Raspberry Sauce make this dessert a crowning glory. It is beautiful, delicious and surprisingly easy.

Planning:
May be made up to 24 hours in advance
Raspberry Sauce must be chilled 2 hours

Preparation Time:
15 minutes

Cooking Time:
1½ hours

Yield:
8 servings

PAVLOVA:

4   egg whites, at room temperature
⅛   teaspoon salt
1   cup granulated sugar
1   tablespoon cornstarch
1   teaspoon white wine vinegar

1   teaspoon vanilla extract
parchment or brown paper
2   cups heavy cream, whipped but unsweetened
fresh fruit (kiwi, bananas, strawberries, etc.)
Raspberry Sauce, if desired

RASPBERRY SAUCE:

1   10-ounce package frozen raspberries
¼   cup granulated sugar

2   teaspoons cornstarch
⅓   cup cold water

PAVLOVA:

- Preheat oven to 400°.
- Beat egg whites and salt together until frothy using an electric mix-er at highest speed. Add all but one tablespoon sugar gradually (2 tablespoons per minute) to the egg whites.
- Mix last tablespoon of sugar with cornstarch and add to whites along with the vinegar and vanilla.
- Beat until stiff peaks form.
- Cover a baking sheet with parchment or brown paper. Shape the meringue into a 7- or 9-inch circle, mounding slightly, on the paper-covered sheet.

continued

- Place in the hot oven and immediately reduce temperature to 250°.
- Bake for 1½ hours. Remove from the oven and cool. Expect the meringue to be lightly browned. It will crack after you remove from the oven and the cooling process takes place.
- If not serving immediately, wrap meringue carefully in plastic wrap and store up to 24 hours at room temperature.
- At serving time, place meringue on a serving plate and spread the whipped cream over the top of meringue. Garnish with fruit. (This is very pretty in concentric circles of different fruits.)
- Optional Raspberry Sauce can be drizzled over the top or spooned on each serving.

RASPBERRY SAUCE:
- Force berries through a sieve to remove seeds.
- Combine sugar, cornstarch and water in a saucepan. Mix well.
- Add sieved berries and cook, stirring constantly until the sauce is thick. Chill.

Chocolate Truffles

Rich and chocolaty, these truffles are perfect for the holidays.

Planning:
Refrigerate mixture at least 4 hours prior to rolling.

Preparation Time:
1 hour (this is mostly spent in rolling the truffles)

Refrigeration Time:
At least 4 hours

Yield:
50 to 75 truffles

8   ounces semi-sweet chocolate
8   ounces unsweetened chocolate (8 squares)
4   cups confectioners' sugar
2   yolks from large eggs

1½ cups unsalted butter at room temperature
4 to 6 tablespoons rum
chopped nuts, cocoa, or powdered sugar to roll the truffles in

- Melt chocolates and let cool to room temperature.
- While the chocolate cools, mix together the sugar, egg yolks, butter and rum until fluffy with an electric mixer.
- Add the chocolate to the sugar mixture and mix thoroughly.
- Refrigerate overnight or at least 4 hours.
- Shape into bite-sized balls and roll in nuts, cocoa, or powdered sugar.

Note: Truffles may be frozen. The mixture may also be made ahead, stored in the freezer and rolled as needed.

Planning:
May be prepared in advance

Preparation Time:
30 minutes

Cooking Time:
10 to 20 minutes

Yield:
25 pieces

Presidential Pralines

Courtesy of Barbara Bush, our First Lady
Perfect for the holiday candy bowl

1   **pound light brown sugar**
1   **5-ounce can evaporated milk (¾ cup)**

1   **cup pecan halves (may be chopped)**

- Mix all ingredients together in a heavy saucepan. Cook over moderately hot heat stirring until dissolved. Heat until mixture forms a soft ball in cold water, approximately 10 to 20 minutes. (If using a candy thermometer, boil until mixture reaches 240°.)

- Remove from heat and let mixture stand for about 5 minutes, then beat until it begins to thicken.

- Drop tablespoonsful onto wax paper. Let harden. If the pralines begin to harden before they spread, add a small amount of hot water or warm over heat for a minute or two.

Note: Store in an airtight container up to 2 weeks or freeze until needed.

Painted Christmas Cookies

This cookie dough recipe is nice as it is not too sweet and doesn't require any refrigeration before rolling. Don't just think of these cookies at Christmas time. They are wonderful in any season depending on the cookie cutters.

Planning:
You will need a number of paintbrushes for painting. The kind that young children use with watercolors is ideal.

Preparation Time:
1½ hours, includes cutting and baking time

Painting Time:
1 to 2 hours depending on complexity of design and number of "painters" enjoying the project.

Cooking Time:
8 to 10 minutes

Yield:
50 to 70 cookies, depending on size of cutters

3 cups flour	1 egg
½ teaspoon baking powder	2 teaspoons vanilla
⅛ teaspoon salt	⅛ teaspoon ground nutmeg
1 cup butter, softened	(optional)
½ cup sugar	

ICING:

3 egg whites	3 cups confectioners' sugar
3 tablespoons lemon juice	food coloring

- Preheat oven to 375°.
- Sift flour, baking powder and salt together.
- Cream butter and sugar together with an electric mixer until light in color.
- Add egg and vanilla extract and optional nutmeg, beating until mixture is light and fluffy.
- Add sifted dry ingredients to the butter mixture. Mix on low speed just until combined.
- On a floured board, roll dough to a thickness of ⅛-inch and cut with cookie cutters. Place cookies on an ungreased cookie sheet and bake for 8 to 10 minutes, or until edges are lightly browned. Cool on a rack.

continued

- Mix all Icing ingredients, except food coloring, together in a bowl. Divide into 5 or 6 smaller bowls. Tint each bowl with different colors of food coloring.
- Paint designs on the cookies with small brushes. After a little practice, anyone, even small children, will be producing terrific cookies. For very fine details (Santa's whiskers, outline, etc.) let the base color dry a bit before painting the detailing. Allow the cookies to dry on a rack before storing.

Note: Painting cookies is a fun activity for a children's birthday party. Just divide the frosting up into numerous paper cups and provide plenty of paint brushes.

Planning:
Requires 30 to 45 minutes of chilling

Preparation Time:
15 minutes, including rolling time

Cooking Time:
20 to 30 minutes

Yield:
24 to 30 cookies

Mexican Wedding Cakes

These melt-in-your-mouth cookies are an excellent choice for an afternoon tea or your holiday cookie jar.

½   **pound butter, softened**
½   **cup confectioners' sugar**
2   **cups sifted flour**
1   **teaspoon vanilla**

1   **cup chopped pecans or walnuts**
confectioners' sugar, for rolling

- Preheat oven to 350°.
- With an electric mixer, cream the butter and sugar until fluffy.
- Add flour, vanilla and nuts. Mix together by hand.
- Chill batter 30 to 45 minutes.
- Roll into small balls or form into crescents.
- Bake on ungreased cookie sheet 20 to 30 minutes or until delicately browned.
- Roll in confectioners' sugar while warm.

Brown Sugar Shortbread

The roasted almonds in this shortbread have a great flavor. These are terrific for a picnic.

Planning:
May be made ahead

Preparation Time:
30 minutes

Cooking Time:
15 to 20 minutes plus 30 to 35 minutes

Yield:
16 servings

½   **cup unblanched almonds**
1   **cup sweet butter, softened**
⅔   **cup brown sugar**

2   **cups flour**
⅛   **teaspoon salt**

- Preheat oven to 350°.
- Place almonds on cookie sheet and roast in the oven for 15 to 20 minutes. (Watch carefully after 10 minutes to avoid overbrowning.) Remove almonds to cool and reduce the oven temperature to 300°.
- Cream together butter and sugar until light and fluffy.
- Add flour and salt and blend by hand until dough is kneadable.
- Knead nuts into dough.
- Divide dough in half. Roll each half into an eight-inch circle ⅓-inch thick on a floured board.
- Place each circle on a buttered baking sheet. Crimp the edges of each circle. Score each one into eight wedges and prick with a fork for decoration.
- Bake for 30 to 35 minutes until brown. Let cool. Cut and serve.

Preparation Time:
15 minutes

Cooking Time:
25 minutes

Yield:
10 to 12 servings

Chocolate Shortbread Divine

This is a rich, satisfying dessert easily prepared.

2	cups flour
1/4	teaspoon salt
1/4	teaspoon baking soda
1/4	teaspoon baking powder
1/2	cup sugar
1	cup margarine or butter, softened
2	egg yolks
1	teaspoon water
1	teaspoon vanilla
1	6-ounce package of semi-sweet chocolate chips
2	egg whites
1/2	cup brown sugar

- Preheat oven to 350°.
- Sift flour, salt, baking soda, and baking powder.
- In another bowl, mix the sugar, margarine or butter, and egg yolks. Add the flour mixture along with water and vanilla.
- Grease a 9-inch square pan. Spread the mixture along the bottom of the pan.
- Sprinkle the chocolate chips on top of mixture.
- With an electric mixer, beat the two egg whites until stiff while adding the brown sugar gradually. Spread egg white mixture over top of the chocolate chips.
- Bake for 25 minutes.

Almost Mrs. Fields Cookies

Preparation Time:
30 minutes

Cooking Time:
8 minutes per cookie sheet

Yield:
11 dozen

This is a recipe many of us have dreamed of finding.

1	pound butter, softened	5	cups uncooked oatmeal (may be ground in a food processor)
2	cups brown sugar		
2	cups white sugar		
4	eggs, beaten	3	cups chopped nuts
2	teaspoons vanilla extract	24	ounces chocolate chips
2	teaspoons baking powder	1	8-ounce chocolate candy bar, grated (optional)
2	teaspoons baking soda		
4½	cups sifted flour		

- Preheat oven to 350°.
- With an electric mixer, cream butter and sugars together in a large bowl.
- Add beaten eggs and vanilla. Beat well.
- Mix together baking powder, baking soda and flour. Blend into sugar mixture.
- Stir in oatmeal (ground or unground), nuts, chocolate chips and the optional grated chocolate bar.
- Roll the dough into 2-inch balls.
- Place 2 inches apart on ungreased cookie sheets.
- Bake for 8 minutes. Remove to a rack and cool.

Note: This recipe may be cut in half very successfully.

Oat Bran Cookies

Preparation Time:
20 minutes

Cooking Time:
8 to 10 minutes per cookie tray

Yield:
5 dozen

A healthier cookie to make for your family.

1 cup flour	1 cup brown sugar (packed)
½ teaspoon baking soda	¼ cup granulated sugar
½ teaspoon salt	1 egg
¼ teaspoon baking powder	1 teaspoon vanilla
½ teaspoon cinnamon	1 cup bran flakes
½ cup butter or margarine, softened	1 cup oatmeal (quick cooking)

- Preheat oven to 350°.
- Sift together the flour, baking soda, salt, baking powder and cinnamon.
- In a large bowl, cream the butter or margarine and sugars with an electric mixer.
- Add egg and vanilla. Beat well.
- Mix in bran flakes and oatmeal. Mix in the dry ingredients. Dough will be quite thick at this point.
- Drop by teaspoons onto a greased cookie sheet 3 inches apart. Flatten each cookie with a spatula dipped in COLD water until very thin.
- Bake 8 to 10 minutes or until lightly browned. Remove from baking sheet while warm to a rack. Cookies will get crisp as they cool.

Chocolate Walnut Meringues

Preparation Time:
15 minutes

Cooking Time:
10 minutes

Yield:
24 to 36 cookies

Light and nutty, these cookies are a delicious accompaniment to ice cream.

2 egg whites, room temperature
½ cup sugar
1 6-ounce package semi-sweet chocolate chips

1 cup chopped walnuts
½ teaspoon vanilla extract

- Preheat oven to 350°.
- With an electric mixer, beat egg whites with sugar until stiff. Set aside.
- Melt chocolate chips in a double boiler. Cool slightly.
- Fold chocolate, nuts, and vanilla into the beaten egg whites.
- Drop mixture from a teaspoon 2 inches apart on a buttered cookie sheet. Bake for 10 minutes being careful not to overbrown.
- Cool on racks. Store in an airtight container.

Preparation Time:
30 minutes

Cooking Time:
40 minutes

Yield:
36 bars

Lemon-Cashew Squares

Indulge in cashews with a smooth lemon glaze.

DOUGH:
½ cup butter, softened
¼ cup sugar
1 egg

1¼ cups flour
½ teaspoon vanilla

TOPPING:
2 eggs, beaten
1½ cups brown sugar
1½ cups chopped roasted
    cashew nuts (unsalted)

2 tablespoons flour
½ teaspoon baking powder
½ teaspoon salt
1 teaspoon vanilla

LEMON GLAZE:
1 cup sugar
⅓ cup milk
2 tablespoons butter or
    margarine

¼ teaspoon salt
1½ teaspoons grated lemon
    rind

- Preheat oven to 350°.
- For DOUGH: cream butter and sugar well. Beat in egg. Add flour and vanilla. Spread into a greased 9 x 13-inch pan. Bake for 15 minutes.
- Mix together all the TOPPING ingredients and spread evenly over baked dough. Return to the oven and bake an additional 25 minutes.
- While squares are cooling, make LEMON GLAZE: place sugar, milk, butter or margarine and salt in a saucepan. Bring to a boil over medium heat and allow to boil for 1 minute. Cool to lukewarm, stir in lemon rind. Drizzle the glaze on squares in an attractive pattern.
- When glaze has set, cut into squares.

Big Apple Squares

Delicious after apple picking as snack or dessert.

Preparation Time:
15 minutes

Cooking Time:
1 hour

Yield:
16 to 18 squares

4 cups peeled and sliced apples	2 teaspoons vanilla
1¾ cups sugar	2 cups flour
2 eggs	2 teaspoons baking powder
½ cup vegetable oil	2 teaspoons cinnamon
	1 teaspoon salt

- Preheat oven to 350°.
- Grease a 9x13x2-inch baking dish.
- Mix apples and sugar and set aside.
- In a large bowl, beat eggs. Add oil and vanilla and mix.
- In a separate bowl, mix dry ingredients together.
- Stir flour mixture and apples mixture alternately into egg mixture.
- Spread into baking dish and bake for 1 hour.
- Cool completely and cut into 2-inch squares.

Note: Excellent with ice cream.

Recipe Contributors

Darlene Abney
Jennie Snider Albertson
Robin Elise Allen
Anne Chapman Amato
Ann Ameen
Roberta Arnott
Jeanne Regan Aronson
Colette Asaff
Julia Atkins
Marcia Avallone
Patricia Neilson Bailey
Kathy W. Baker
Tracey Bauer
Marie M. Beringer
Carol Ann Best
Julia J. Blanchard
Wendy J. Blankin
Joan Blatterman
Cathy Nolan Boniello
Anne W. Boucher
Mary Lee Bradley
Lynne Brazill
Carole Brodin
Therese Brosnan
Cary Brown
Janet McLean Buchbinder
Nancy Bullock
Mona Campbell Burger
Mary Barry Burkhardt
Barbara Bush
Wanda Butler
Rita Crosby Cain
Janice Callahan
Jody Campbell
Douglas Campbell, Jr.
Kathy Harrington Caputo
Beth Casey
Barbara Childs
Betsy Chisholm
Renee Chmiel
Suzanne C. Coleman
Winifred Comlossy
Anne Noone Connolly
Meighan W. Corbett
Susana Corning
Susan D. Corning
Gay Meighan Corning
Joanne M. Cox
Susan Kemper Coyne
Susan Cronin
Gretchen Kaye Crowley
Betsy Culeman
Janet Delbrook Day
Deborah DeRosa

Cynthia DiCrocco
Birgit Rasmussen DiForio
Nancy M. Diao
Terry Hartnagle Donnellan
Carolyn L. Doubek
Bunny Douek
Genevieve Hellier DuVerneuil
Suzanne Emery
Dorothy Ennis
Maryann Errigo
Terry B. Fadrhonc
Eileen Brennan Ferrell
Rosita Fichtel
Mrs. Roy A. Foulke, Jr.
Sabrina Fox
Bonnie Gagliardi
Julie Gale
Kathryn Gamble
Shirley Ann Ganchou
Susan Gane
Lorraine Garman
Maura Garrabrant
Karen B. Gause
Peter A. Gerardi
Dona Gibbs
Laura Greilsamer
Elizabeth Guerin
Ann Gunsalus
Virginia Giuliano Gunther
Carol Gyllenhoff
Kay Hackley
Sharon Halverson
Nancy Haneman
Christine Haney
Russell Hastings
Terrie Ewbank Henry
Caryl H. Herson
Lois Kuhn Hopson
Ann Horbaczewski
Sandra Thomas Horsman
Glenda W. Hughes
Charlotte B. Hunt
Patricia C. Hyland
Emily Scott Irving
Pamela H. Isom
Martha Crosby Jacobs
Mary A. Jacobson
Tyler Jenner
Lucy Moore Johanson
Joan Kearney
Elsie Kearns
Carolyn Keller
Mary Cecilia Kelly
Lisa B. Kennedy

continued on next page

279

Stephanie H. King
Ann Kirkham
Doree G. Kluss
Carleen Lyden Kluss
Sheila Lahey
Jane Land
Kathleen K. Langer
Kathy Lawrie
Jay Leno
Lisa Liss
Charleen Thompson Livingstone
Ann Luedke Lobdell
Stephanie U. Lord
Joan Gaestel Macfarlane
Maureen Maloney
Marjorie Manley
Lise Claire Martin
Alice P. Matsen
Hilary Healey Matson
Amy McCarthy
Cathy McCarthy
Marsha McCormick
Eileen O. McCorry
Katherine R. McCurdy
Susan M. McDonnell
Ronnie McGovern
Kristy G. McKeon
Rita McKeon
Wendy Megroz
Paula Carroll Meighan
Jennifer Evans Montgomery
Susan Currie Morehouse
Louise Morganstern
Cindy Morris
Gaye Moyse
Angie Nastasi
Ann Nealon
Mary Ann Brennan Newcomb
Audrey H. Olson
Linda Otness
Treacey Galway Owen
Chris Pagnani
Lee Lee Copeland Panno
Margaret M. Parchen
Hilary Bedford Parkhurst
Muffy Pepper
Rona Perkel
Marina Perna
Nancy J. Perone
Suzie Phillips
Sonia M. Pierson
Nancy Clary Pitcairn
Peggy Preisser
Jackie Beach Purcell
Patsy S. Rafter
Margaret D. Raney

Janet Cullinan Raske
Diana L.D. Regan
Rebecca Reisman
Nancy Richy
Dorothy Robertshaw
Sharon F. Robinson
Mary B. Roe
Holly M. Rogers
Maureen Rooney
Mary Gray Sachtjen
Vivi Samaladas
Paula Saunders
Carol Scheffler
Adrienne W. Scott
Randi Season
Andrew H. Sharp
Carol Shields
Joanne Siddons
Betty Siegal
Shiranne Simmons
Andrea Sporer Simon
Mary Skoyles
Penelope S. Smith
Janet Igler Smith
Sarah Soong
Barbara Dempsey Spelman
Barbara Schultz Spencer
Anne Goode Stalker
Betsy Livingstone Steers
Judy H. Steers
Marion Stewart
Pamela Stone
Maud Gaines Tarrant
Dyanne D. Thompson
Kimberley Thompson
Marcy Trenholm
Nora Tulchin
Jane Turk
Helen Utz
Jeanne Van Valen
Christina Van Wagenen
Betsy Wadsworth
Janet S. Walker
Joan Walsh
Janet S. Walter
Hilary H. Watson
Margaret Wieland
Edna Wilkes
Lois Wilkin
Diane Wanderer Williams
Louise Wolf
Lucy Yocum
Leslie B. York
Carol Young
Lisa Hotte Young

Index